The World of
Goya

TIME LIFE BOOKS ®

TIME-LIFE LIBRARY OF ART

The World of Goya

1746-1828

by Richard Schickel
and
the Editors of TIME-LIFE BOOKS

TIME-LIFE BOOKS, New York

About the Author

Richard Schickel is a journalist who has turned a critical eye on both popular culture and the fine arts. Best known as LIFE's film critic, he is the author of several books, including a social history, a story for children and four volumes of film history and criticism, the latest of which is a perceptive analysis of the life, times and art of Walt Disney, called *The Disney Version*. A former Guggenheim Fellow, Mr. Schickel is a graduate of the University of Wisconsin. Long fascinated by the blending of realism and fantasy in Goya's art, he traveled to Spain in research for this book.

The Consulting Editor

H. W. Janson is Professor of Fine Arts at New York University, where he is also Chairman of the Department of Fine Arts at Washington Square College. Among his numerous publications are his *History of Art* and *The Sculpture of Donatello*.

The Consultant for This Book

Priscilla Muller, Curator of Paintings at the Hispanic Society of America in New York City, has taught Baroque art at Brooklyn College and has lectured at numerous institutions. She is the author of many articles and reviews on Spanish art. Dr. Muller is a Corresponding Member of the *Real Academia de Ciencias, Bellas Letras y Nobles Artes de Córdoba* and an honorary member of the Spanish Institute in New York.

On the Slipcase

Goya's portrait of the aristocratic Spanish beauty Doña Isabel Cobos de Porcel is supposed to have been his gift of gratitude for the hospitality he received from the lady and her husband during his stay at their home.

End Papers

Front: A preparatory drawing for Goya's last series of etchings, *Disparates,* depicts a frenzied yet rhythmic dance in which three coquettish women and three fat, drunken men seem transformed into puppets.
Back: In this preparatory drawing, also for the *Disparates,* the terror of a gigantic figure, a familiar feature in Goya's fantastic world, is juxtaposed with the panic that confronts fleeing soldiers.

TIME-LIFE BOOKS

EDITOR
Jerry Korn
EXECUTIVE EDITOR
A. B. C. Whipple
PLANNING DIRECTOR
Oliver E. Allen
TEXT DIRECTOR   ART DIRECTOR
Martin Mann   Sheldon Cotler
CHIEF OF RESEARCH
Beatrice T. Dobie
DIRECTOR OF PHOTOGRAPHY
Melvin L. Scott
Associate Planning Director: Byron Dobell
Assistant Text Directors:
Ogden Tanner, Diana Hirsh
Assistant Art Director: Arnold C. Holeywell
Assistant Chief of Research: Martha T. Goolrick

PUBLISHER
Joan D. Manley
General Manager: John D. McSweeney
Business Manager: John Steven Maxwell
Sales Director: Carl G. Jaeger
Promotion Director: Paul R. Stewart
Public Relations Director: Nicholas Benton

TIME-LIFE LIBRARY OF ART

SERIES EDITOR: Robert Morton
Associate Editor: Diana Hirsh
Editorial Staff for *The World of Goya:*
Picture Editor: Jane Scholl
Designer: Paul Jensen
Staff Writers: James MaHood,
Paula Norworth, John von Hartz
Chief Researcher: Martha Turner
Researchers: Judith Levenson, Ann McLeod,
Rosemary O'Connell, Susanna Seymour
Art Assistant: Mervyn Clay

EDITORIAL PRODUCTION
Production Editor: Douglas B. Graham
Quality Director: Robert L. Young
Assistant: James J. Cox
Copy Staff: Rosalind Stubenberg, Laurie LaMartine, Florence Keith
Picture Department: Dolores A. Littles, Suzanne Jaffe, Barbara S. Simon

The following individuals and departments of Time Inc. helped to produce this book: Editorial Production, Norman Airey, Margaret T. Fischer; Library, Peter Draz; Picture Collection, Doris O'Neil; Photographic Laboratory, George Karas; TIME-LIFE News Service, Murray J. Gart; Correspondents Maria Vincenza Aloisi (Paris), Jean Bratton (Madrid), Alex des Fontaines (Geneva), Margot Hapgood (London) and Ann Natanson (Rome).

Contents

Fran.^{co} Goya y Lucientes
Pintor.

I

Painter of the Spanish Mind

The Prado Museum in Madrid contains the greatest collection of Spanish art in the world. But it is something more than the treasury of a nation's artistic patrimony. It is also a microcosm where one confronts, in all its infuriating contradictions, that historical and spiritual enigma, the Spanish character.

Spain's artists have served it well, recording with extraordinary force and clarity the principal components of their country's nature. The works of the three greatest are arrayed on the Prado's second floor, where a long, narrow gallery gives access to a series of smaller rooms and culminates in a rotunda. The visitor comes first to El Greco, who was born a Greek, but adopted Spain as his homeland. Better than any native, he captured on canvas the spiritual aspiration of the Spanish soul. A poet speaks of the "winged hands" of his figures, an art historian of their "elongated, spiraling bodies [that] soared to heaven"; everyone mentions their eyes, yearning for another world and haunted by the sins of this one. What animates El Greco is the religious idealism that animated the imperial designs of the Spanish crown in his time. His art is the shaft of pure light whose radiance illuminates the darkness that followed so quickly when that ideal failed.

Farther along the Prado's second floor is El Greco's great successor Velázquez, painter of Spain's worldly pride and power, of the pomp and panoply of that brief moment in the 17th Century when the nation stood boldly, if insecurely, at the center of the historical stage. He, like his country, is confident of his power—a serene realist, sure of his vision, his technical mastery, his place in the life of his times. Like El Greco, he painted saints and Madonnas, but somehow they seem perfunctory compared to his majestic series of royal portraits, his grand visions of high historical moments. There is richness and ease in the manner of his subjects. And yet, shadows lie across most of his canvases, as if Velázquez sensed what his sitters did not—that the tide had turned against Spain, that the royal spectacle he recorded with such faithful brilliance was both illusion and delusion. With Velázquez's death, darkness begins to descend on Spanish art.

From Velázquez the Prado visitor passes on to the last of Spain's triumvirate of old masters, Francisco José de Goya y Lucientes. His works fill the small rotunda to which the museum's main gallery leads as to a climax. An untidy, prolific man, he alone of the three cannot be contained on this floor. Much of his art has overflowed to a warren of darker rooms downstairs, and there is something appropriate about that. For if El Greco was the painter of Spanish spirituality and Velázquez the painter of her pride, then Goya is the painter of her anarchical individualism; the stubborn, basic unruliness of the Spanish mind. No one better than Goya evokes the unique Spanish pessimism about man's fallen state. It is a feeling so profound as to preclude all faith in political, social or economic progress, and ordained to regard all temporal leaders, theories and organizations, especially governments, as irrelevant at best and comically tragic (or tragically comic) at worst. His two great predecessors offer visions of the things that sustain the Spanish temperament. Goya completes the picture by offering a vision of the things that torment it—of its heart of darkness.

There are no saints in Goya's room and no heroes either—only mortals whose desires are all too clearly confined to the petty vanities of the world. The rotunda contains the two most popular paintings Goya ever did—the clothed and the nude *Majas*—but it is dominated by his portrait of the royal family of Charles IV *(pages 72-75)*, the Bourbon king later deposed by Napoleon. In the arrangement of its subjects, the painting owes much to Velázquez, but in place of cool objectivity there is a subjective passion in this work that brings it close to caricature. Standing before it not long before he died, Ernest Hemingway said: "Is it not a masterpiece of loathing? Look how he has painted his spittle into every face. Can you imagine that he had such genius that he could fulfill this commission and please the King, who, because of his fatuousness, could not see how Goya had stamped him for all the world to see?"

It was easy for Hemingway—or for any other citizen of today—to imagine this kind of engaged yet duplicitous genius. Goya's time in Spanish history—the late 18th and early 19th Centuries—was a period very like the present, a period when all illusions had been abandoned and the air was charged by the spirit of radical change. The effects of such a climate are well known. Disorientation, alienation, fragmentation, despair, these are, for the individual, the seemingly inevitable by-products of sweeping attempts at social realignment, and they are Goya's real subject, whether he is painting kings or commoners. More properly, they are half of his subject. The other half is himself—his response to the emotions he saw in the faces around him and felt in his own tormented mind. This subjectivity, the tendency to value the uniqueness and originality of the individual artist's vision over all rules and dogma lies at the heart of the modern spirit in art. It is another reason why the shock of recognition on first encountering Goya is so great. "Goya believed in movement," Hemingway continued, ". . . in everything he ever experienced and *felt*. You don't look at Goya if you want neutrality."

Precisely. There is none in *The Family of Charles IV*. But Goya's life until approximately the time of this painting had been a struggle to preserve his neutrality. And he had succeeded. The best commissions were his for the asking; he was, indeed, "First Painter to the King" when he undertook the family portrait. It was the culmination of a public career the naked ambitiousness of which has few parallels in the history of art. *The Family of Charles IV* is the pivot of his career, the work in which the public Goya and the private Goya—so rigidly separated before and after this moment of truth—were briefly allowed to merge. Perhaps this is why the Prado's place of honor belongs to it. For if Goya's career turns on this work then we are studying the results of the first public confrontation between a modern artist and modern history.

"With him you have the beginnings of our modern anarchy," Bernard Berenson said when he viewed an exhibition of Goya's work. "And now modern painting begins," André Malraux declared at the end of his study of the Spaniard. And we agree. Effort is required to appreciate El Greco's warm spirituality, Velázquez's cool objectivity. But we feel Goya in our bones and in our blood. We know him, or think we know him, as instinctively as we know ourselves.

There is, however, a certain irony in this easy understanding of Goya, for little is known of the facts of his life. The desire to preserve biographical documents is not highly developed in Spain. History is something the Spaniard lives, not something he cares to ponder in a systematic way. And so there is almost no reliable evidence about the shaping years of Goya's life—his first quarter of a century is largely a blank in the historical record, a blank on which we project the shadow of the man he was to become, not the firm outlines of the youth he really was.

One of the few known facts about him is the exact place and date of his birth—in the village of Fuendetodos in the province of Aragon on March 30, 1746. The records of the parish church reveal that much, at least. We know, too, that he grew up with no loyalties more extensive than those he naturally granted to his family, village community and his church. This independence of larger loyalties—to the national state, to the world beyond his particular horizon— was the birthright of every Spaniard in Goya's time. It had its roots in geography—a random distribution of mountain ranges divides Spain into a series of regions vastly different in climate, terrain, produce and, therefore, character. Spain's regions had long resisted such attempts as were made to weld them together into a true nation and, at the time of Goya's birth, the monarchy, preoccupied by foreign adventures, had abandoned the effort. Spain, one of Goya's contemporaries wrote, was "a body composed of other and smaller bodies, separated and in opposition to one another, which oppress and despise each other and are in a continuous state of war." This ancient tradition of isolationism was fatalistically accepted by most Spaniards.

In 1700, just 46 years before Goya's birth, the last of the Spanish Habsburg monarchs, Charles II (or "Charles the Bewitched" as he was popularly known), had finally died. With him died whatever fantasy of a Golden Age had persisted, for "this disgusting, but pitiful creature," as one historian described him, seemed to symbolize in his very person the decay of the Spanish empire. An epileptic, underdeveloped in size and

In 1746 Goya was born in the desolate Spanish village of Fuendetodos, shown in the photograph above. Located in the northeastern province of Aragon, the town is surrounded by a rocky, hilly and hot countryside and contains fewer inhabitants today—about 100—than it did during Goya's time. The two-story stone house that was his birthplace is preserved as a Goya memorial in Fuendetodos; in the photograph below it is framed by an arcade.

grotesque in physiognomy, his cretinous mind was more feeble than his body. No one had expected him to outlive his childhood but, cruelly for himself and for Spain, he survived and reigned without ruling for 35 years—years wasted by his court in endless plottings for succession, since it was obvious that he could produce no heir. One party, led by Charles' mother, favored continuation of rule by relatives of the Austrian royal family. The opposing French party advanced the candidacy of Louis XIV's grandson, Philip of Anjou, who, through his Spanish grandmother, had a much weaker hereditary claim. Since the two countries had gone to war four times during Charles' reign, with Spain the loser in each instance, France had a poor propaganda position as well. French diplomatic skills, however, easily compensated for these deficiencies. One by one, officials who favored Austrian succession were supplanted in the King's favor by men favoring the French cause. Their intrigues intruded even into his death chamber where, at last, Charles was persuaded to name the Bourbon Prince Philip as his successor. "God be praised!" a Spaniard was heard to exclaim. "The Pyrenees have disappeared. Now we are all one."

But it was not to be that easy for the French-born Philip—or for Spain. His accession to the throne as Philip V created an alliance between France and Spain that shifted a balance of power that had pertained on the continent for over a century. In 1700 Philip was forced to fight to defend his crown against the Austrians, who had no intention of playing the role of graceful losers in what they justifiably regarded as an unfair struggle for power in Spain. The Austrians enlisted as allies the English, the Dutch and the House of Savoy, most powerful of the Italian states—all interested in maintaining the old power-balancing division between France and Spain and in picking off bargain bits of the Spanish empire. The allies, moreover, found supporters within Spain in the chronically disaffected province of Catalonia. For more than a decade, Spain was a bloody battlefield, and the war further reduced the wretched countryside. Peace was finally bought dearly. Philip formally surrendered Gibraltar and Minorca to Britain and the Catholic Netherlands—Flanders and Luxembourg—along with the majority of Spain's Italian possessions to Austria.

It has been observed by historians that, had Philip not been a weak and easily misled man, he might have seen these terms as a boon instead of a penalty. Charles E. Chapman, an American historian of Spain, characterized the entire reign of the old Habsburg monarchs this way: "Spain wasted her energies and expended her wealth in a fruitless attempt, first to become the dominant power in Europe, and later to maintain possessions in Italy and the Low Countries which were productive only of trouble; what she took from the Americas with the one hand, she squandered in Europe with the other." Had Philip seen this he might have changed history's course by avoiding a repetition of his predecessors' mistakes. He still controlled most of Latin America, which produced enormous wealth in gold and raw materials. Instead of wasting this treasure on the preposterous dream of European empire, the wealth might have regenerated the land.

Unfortunately, Philip let the opportunity slip. In 1714, when the War of the Spanish Succession finally ended, his first wife, Maria Luisa of Savoy, died. A spirited and courageous woman, she had been unwavering in her loyalty to her adopted land, although her father had joined the alliance against Spain. Inspired by her example, the Spaniards—always excepting the independent Catalans—had rallied to Philip and the national cause in a way that was quite exceptional for them. Philip's love for Maria Luisa, alas, led him into a disastrous error; he assumed that all Italian noblewomen were equally well-favored, and so he took another one, Isabel Farnese of Parma, as his second wife. She was intelligent and extremely ambitious, and it was not long before both qualities were obsessively directed toward securing Italian realms for her sons to rule. Thus, the well-intentioned Philip found himself embroiled once again in a series of imperial wars. None of them were waged on Spanish soil, and not all of them were fought, indeed, in Italy. But all grew out of his wife's manueverings for position in that country. Ultimately, she achieved her aims (and earned the sobriquet, "Termagent of Spain"), although it required the rest of her husband's reign—and years more—before Naples was acquired for her firstborn, the duchies of Parma, Piacenza and Guastalla for her second. In the meantime, the neglect of the Spanish land and people continued unabated as all the wealth of the American colonies—not to mention the nation's best talents—was directed toward foreign intrigues.

The degree of this neglect is reflected in a few simple facts. In the year of Goya's birth, for example, the capital city of Madrid had no centrally organized refuse collection and no coherent street lighting or cleaning service. The police force was lackadaisical in the cities and virtually unknown in the countryside, where banditry was a well-recognized danger. This was made even easier by the fact that the Spanish road system was almost totally undeveloped. Rutted and bumpy roads not only slowed travelers, who became the bandits' prey, but also made pursuit of the thieves difficult. This lack of the most elementary services and protections was only the beginning of the national government's deficiencies. There was no systematic attempt at education by the government, little encouragement of agricultural reforms and few innovations in industrial or mercantile methods. Before 1746 state intervention in these areas was largely aimed at protecting existing privileges, not at reform. Whatever prosperity existed was concentrated at the periphery of the nation in such maritime trading centers as Cádiz and Barcelona. In the central agricultural regions—Aragon, La Mancha, Castile—however, poverty was dire and continuous. Vast landholdings by the Church and by a handful of noble families were worked by tenant farmers who received no more than subsistence wages. Few farmers took any interest in the intelligent management of agriculture—crop rotation and irrigation, for example— and the quality of a land none too bountiful to begin with grew worse with each passing year.

Then, too, the nation had to contend with the reactionary attitudes of the Church and the aristocracy. Catholicism was more than a religion in Spain; it was the major force in society. Indeed, it was the only force

The interior of the house in Fuendetodos where Goya was born has been restored and decorated with 18th Century furnishings typical of those in small-town artisans' homes of the period. The bedroom in the foreground and the living room beyond probably look much as they did when the artist lived there. Guides make the dubious claim that Goya was born in this very bed and that he owned the embroidered blouse spread across it.

Fuendetodos, Goya's birthplace, is situated on Spain's arid central plateau, among lands denuded, like half the country, by centuries of overgrazing. Schooled in Aragon's capital, Saragossa, Goya tasted luxury at the rich estate of his first royal patron, the Infante Don Luis, in Arenas de San Pedro. He knew agonizing illness in the port city of Cádiz, delight with the Duchess of Alba in her Sanlúcar hideaway, triumph and disillusion in Madrid.

most people recognized. As such, the Church might ideally have provided the social organization and the intellectual drive that the Spanish crown was unable to supply. But the Church did not. Ruled by a top-heavy bureaucracy, it provided far too many parish priests in the countryside. They were often ill-prepared for their work or forced to exist without benefice, and their support was a drain on both the populace and the Church. Finally, through the Inquisition, the Church laid a heavy hand on the intellectual life of Spain. Founded by the Pope in 1235, the Inquisition had long and vigorously been concerned with the suppression of heresy. And although in succeeding centuries the power of the Holy Office waxed and waned, depending on the attitudes of sovereigns who could manipulate its activities, it was always there. No Spanish intellectual or artist could be sure that the Inquisition would not spring suddenly to life and haul him before one of its tribunals to question his work or even his reading habits.

The aristocracy was, if anything, less helpful than the Church. Its prejudice against "useful" work had rendered it socially impotent and, indeed, blind to the misery that supported its style of life. Idleness was the principal symbol of its status and to work, even as a gentleman farmer, was considered *déclassé*. The most powerful nobles were exempt from many taxes and military obligations. Furthermore, they enjoyed monopoly privileges in certain vital economic areas. One of the most destructive of these monopolies was the *Mesta*, the powerful sheep ranchers' association. Since the 13th Century, the *Mesta* had enjoyed a wide use of some of the best land in Spain. *Mesta*-owned sheep ate their way across fields and farms, destroying crops and pasturage needed by other animals. In the process, the royally sanctioned *Mesta* ended any hope Spain had of a rational agriculture—and there was no appealing its decisions.

No force in Spanish society was capable of counterbalancing power of this kind. The middle class was insignificant, and the crafts were still organized on the basis of the medieval guild system, preventing the growth of a modern entrepreneurial class. The professions—law and medicine—had achieved none of the status and influence that they enjoyed elsewhere in Europe. Finally, since there was no significant industrial organization, there was no energetic proletariat to contribute a revolutionary yeast to the social brew.

In short, Spain, until the time of Goya's birth and childhood, was a stagnant, if not decadent, social organism. This fact—and the certainty that no one with authority cared enough to do anything about it—was a basic condition of life in Spain in the first part of the 18th Century. It was responsible for the quality of life in Goya's native Fuendetodos and in thousands of *pueblos* just like it.

Physically, Fuendetodos was as bleak as the inner lives of its inhabitants. It had no river and scarcely any rainfall. The fields its 109 residents worked in the summers provided no more than a bare living. The crop of the region was wheat, and for a few months of the year the harsh and rocky hills surrounding the village were green with it. But most of the time the unshaded land stood barren, bleaching almost white under the unrelenting sun. The Goya house was scarcely more than a hut, its heavy, dark stone walls broken irregularly by small windows, which gave a view of the dusty road wandering past. The lasting impression this arid country made on Goya is clear in the landscape backgrounds of his work—especially his etchings. They are remarkably empty, with only a gnarled tree or a jagged outcropping of rock breaking the low line of a featureless horizon. The look of the land perfectly matches the bleak lives of the people pictured in the foreground of many of the etchings, but this is more than a stylistic device; it is also a realistic interpretation of the landscape in which, as a boy, Goya was imprisoned.

Poverty and isolation, then, formed the basis of the Spanish temperament in general and Francisco Goya's in particular. They created his stubborn independence and created, as well, the darker side of his nature —his selfishness and his essential loneliness.

There was, however, one important respect in which his circumstances differed from those of the peasantry among whom he passed his boyhood. Goya's father, José, neither began nor ended his life as a farmer. He was the son of a notary—the 18th Century equivalent of a small-town lawyer—a modest position, but one which entitled its holder to inclusion in the lower middle class. José himself had been a gilder in Saragossa, but his wife Doña Gracia Lucientes, was a *hidalgo,* a member of the lowest order of the Spanish nobility. The *hidalgo* class had been created by the Spanish monarchy as a means of raising money. Along with other minor titles, the prefix Don or Doña could be added to one's name simply by putting up a certain amount of cash. By Goya's day there were something like a half-million *hidalgos*—one-twentieth of the population—in Spain. Their lot was not a pleasant one. Custom, rigidly adhered to, forbade members of this class from doing "useful" work—practicing a trade or craft. They were nobles in the feudal sense of the term and therefore expected to live on the income from their "estates."

That is precisely what José Goya undertook to do when his wife inherited her family's land in Fuendetodos. It is a good measure of the Spanish obsession with titles that he may have gone to Fuendetodos at an economic sacrifice even though the title was his wife's and not his own. There, he could act the part of the nobleman, walking "majestically in the sad square of his poor town," as a contemporary poet described his type, "muffled in his bad cloak, contemplating the coat-of-arms above the door of his half-fallen house, giving thanks to God and to Providence for having made him Don So-and-So."

The fantasy, however, could not long endure, and sometime between 1758 and 1760—perhaps even earlier—the Goyas abandoned their dream of status as village gentry and quietly returned to Saragossa, where José resumed his old trade as a gilder. Apparently the move had little effect on his prosperity, for when he died in Saragossa some years later, the official record of that event bore the brief, poignant notation that "he died without leaving a will, because he had nothing whatever."

The move, however, certainly had a tremendous effect on Francisco. Saragossa was, after all, a provincial capital, and in its narrow, dark and crooked streets there thrived a life infinitely richer than that of an agricultural village. The city was the prosperous trading and artistic center of Aragon. Since the Middle Ages local painters and sculptors had purveyed religious decorations to the village churches of the region, and Saragossa thus supported a cultural and educational establishment more lively than that of many comparable Spanish cities.

Along with his elder brothers Camillo (who was destined for the priesthood) and Tomás (who followed his father's trade), Francisco entered a rather primitive school run by a Father Joaquin of the teaching Order of Escolopes. The quality of the school was not high; Goya just barely learned to read and write, and his spelling, penmanship and qualities of verbal expression remained coarse throughout his life. The modern Spanish philosopher José Ortega y Gasset once observed that "Goya's letters are those of a carpenter." Even so, the boy received more education than most 18th Century Spaniards of his class. This was at least partly a tribute to his father's ambitions, which he himself was beginning to acquire and which were to drive him throughout his life.

Perhaps the most important thing the school provided Goya was a close friend. He was Martín Zapater, a stable, sensible fellow who remained in Saragossa for the rest of his life. From 1763, when Goya left Saragossa for Madrid, until 1801, when the gap between the two men became unbridgeable, Zapater remained Goya's faithful correspondent, always referred to as "the Good Martín." "I know," Goya once wrote, "that we understand each other in everything, and that God has chosen us in this respect, among so many others, and we thank him for it with all our hearts." Zapater faithfully saved every scrap of Goya's correspondence. Equally important, Zapater served the artist as an emotional balance wheel, patiently soothing his excitements, ministering to his despondencies, acting as a sounding board for ideas and, most remarkably, allowing himself to be used as a bench mark against which Goya—sometimes cruelly and always thoughtlessly—measured his worldly progress.

Zapater had stayed behind at their common starting point, Goya had moved onward and upward, and it pleased him to rejoice in the distances he had traveled from "the Good Martín."

After Goya finished his course at Father Joaquin's school, he went on to a Jesuit "college" in Saragossa. There, Father Pignatelli, a member of a clan of Italian noblemen who represented the age-old ties between the kingdoms of Sicily and Aragon and were the leading landholders of the region, suggested that he develop his natural gift for drawing by studying under one of the local master painters, José Luzán y Martínez. Luzán was heavily patronized by Father Pignatelli's family and maintained a school in his home where Goya studied for four years. From him, he learned the principles of draftsmanship, principally by the traditional means of copying etchings and engravings.

Luzán was a typical third-rank Spanish painter of the period. The Pignatelli had sent him to Naples where he spent several years copying the masters and acquiring a derivative style of his own—"provincialized Rococo," it has been called. At 30, Luzán became a court painter and shortly thereafter he opened his studio in Saragossa. He may not have been a very distinguished artist, but he was a highly regarded citizen, admired for his industriousness and probity. Among the many civic-minded chores he undertook was that of "Reviewer of Unchaste Paintings" for the Inquisition in Saragossa.

A few photographs of this small reliquary cabinet are all that remain of Goya's first known work. Sometime between 1758 and 1760 the apprentice artist adorned the wooden cabinet that was treasured by the parish church in his native hamlet of Fuendetodos. The open doors show a Madonna and Child at left and Goya's own patron saint, Francisco de Paula, at right. Closed, the panels showed the Virgin appearing to St. James. Above the cabinet Goya painted a draped canopy held back by two cherubs. The reliquary was destroyed in 1936, during the Spanish Civil War.

Surprisingly, Goya did not chafe under the endless routine of copying; indeed, he must have relished it, for while working with Luzán, he seems also to have enrolled in a school founded by a local sculptor, Juan Ramírez. There he copied from sculpture and plaster casts—one of the only ways of learning to paint the human anatomy in the Catholic Spain of his day, since painting female nudes from life was strictly forbidden, a punishable offense.

Whatever the merits of the instruction Goya received during his adolescence in Saragossa, he showed himself as little more than an adept copyist, capable of quickly assimilating the techniques of others. He showed little gift, as yet, for expressing his own vision. In this period, however, he did execute his first small commission—decorations for the wooden doors of a reliquary cabinet in the little church in Fuendetodos where he had been baptized. On the outside of the cabinet's doors, below feigned curtains, Goya painted *The Appearance of the Virgin of the Pillar* and, on the inside, portraits of *San Francisco de Paula* and *The Virgin of the Carmen.* When he saw these paintings some 50 years later, Goya exclaimed, "Don't say I painted those!"

Despite his later disavowal of this early work, the job seemed to confirm for Goya the choice of his profession. He obviously enjoyed painting, and he must have thought that he would enjoy the life of an artist. From the example of his teachers and their few successful pupils, moreover, he could see that as an artist he would have a mobility, both physical and social, that was denied to all Spaniards who lacked noble birth. A career as a painter was a way up and out of the provinces, and Goya did not hesitate to take it. At the age of 17, he left Saragossa to test himself in a larger arena—in *the* arena—Madrid.

The Diversity of Genius

Francisco Goya, with his unique genius, captured the soul of Spain in an amazing range of works. A dazzlingly versatile artist, he created etchings and lithographs, and painted cartoons for tapestries, incisive portraits, stirring frescoes and deeply felt scenes of reality and the imagination. Born to a poor family that was only barely genteel, he was endowed with a restless ambition that, coupled with his ennobling gift, carried him to the fashionable world of Madrid and its royal court, where Spain's wealthiest aristocrats became his patrons. He had the vigorous, inflammable nature of a rebel, but his deep need for security and affluence taught him to curb his tongue. Material success and personal prudence, however, never dulled the thrust of his art. He remained to his dying day, at the age of 82, a passionate Spaniard who drew and painted with intense veracity those things he saw around him and the emotion he felt for them.

Goya's zest for living seldom deserted him, even though it was subjected to brutal tests. He suffered two serious illnesses, one of which denied him his hearing at the age of 46. He watched with horror the barbaric Napoleonic wars as they ravaged Spain, and he was witness to sickening displays of ineptitude exhibited by the Spanish rulers in the royal court. But in his fervent sense of humanity and his passion for reason he revealed the concern he felt for his land and his fellow man. With stunning creative energy he transmitted it all to canvas.

This selection of Goya's paintings, drawn from the many styles and techniques with which he experimented in his long career, includes themes as dissimilar as picnics in a park and the brutalities of a madhouse. The details on the following pages will reveal the power of his brush.

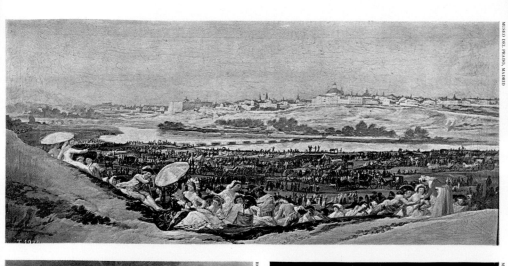

163

Goya's sensitivity to the leisurely pastimes of Spanish everyday life ensured his success as a designer of tapestry cartoons like the *Festival of San Isidro (above)*. Here, residents of Madrid gather in a park across the Manzanares River from the capital to honor Isidro, the city's patron saint. Isidro was a peasant who lived in the 12th Century. One hot day his plow uncovered a fast-flowing stream; four centuries later water from the stream

18

Festival of San Isidro, detail

cured a mysterious illness of the young prince, who later became the powerful monarch, Philip II, and the miraculous cure brought about Isidro's canonization. Every May 15 people gathered to drink the wonder-working water, picnic, sing, dance, exchange visits and pass the wineskins. This painting, one of Goya's last tapestry cartoons, shows his growing deftness in lively composition, energetic brush work and subtle color.

19

The Burial of the Sardine, detail

Atheme that engrossed Goya throughout his life was the similarity between the wild joys of a crowd and the real insanity of truly deranged men. The madness common both at a fiesta and in an asylum is seen in the

two details above from paintings that Goya probably completed during his recuperation from the terrible illness that left him deaf. *The Burial of the Sardine* shows a Spanish ritual in which a sardine, a substitute for a roasted

The Madhouse, detail

pig, is symbolically buried to mark the end of carnival feasting and the beginning of Lent. The wantonness of this last fling before the denials of the Lenten season was not missed by Goya; the grisly masks of the celebrants add to the frantic air. Indeed, the revelers appear no more stable than the men in *The Madhouse.* There, Goya also drives home the frightening similarity between the madmen and the man whose job it is to control them.

21

Witches, hobgoblins and other phantasmagoric creatures have seldom been portrayed more convincingly than by Goya. In paintings such as *The Incantation (right),* which was done, oddly enough, for one of his society patrons, Goya paints these hideous monsters with an almost loving concern. In effect, Goya was painting what was felt by many of the leading minds of the Age of Enlightenment—if witches and their kin exist, they take shape in the forces of unreasoning folly, stupidity and prejudice that threaten the order of the sensible, rational world.

In this painting Goya shows a terrified woman dressed only in a nightgown kneeling before a small group of witches. One of the hags holds a basket of children, one reads by candlelight while another, wearing the headdress made of two bats, jabs a long needle into an infant. The witch in yellow at the center of the painting mutters the incantation over the cowering woman while a demon and a flock of owls hover above them. The precise meaning of this strange painting is unclear; it may have been an illustration of a scene from a popular play. On the other hand, Goya's inspiration could have been the widespread superstition that those who permit themselves to have lustful desires thereby enter a pact with the devil. Thus, the mother, kneeling in her chemise, might be subjecting her babies, born or unborn, to a curse from Satan's representatives in payment for her sins. Goya was to remain fascinated by eerie semihumans, symbolic of irrationality and distorted mental states, all his life; he drew them in his *Caprichos* and *Disparates (pages 108-119)* and in the obsessive images of the "Black Paintings" in his old age *(pages 172-185).*

The Incantation, detail

Majas on a Balcony, detail

Goya's capacity to evoke beauty pervades these two canvases. At left, his subject is the young son of an aristocrat, elegantly outfitted. But the fancy clothes do not distinguish the boy; the warm glow of the child's innocence does. Goya's compassion for children is self-evident, but it does not smother his sense of humor—the three cats hungrily watch the pet bird on the string; the card in the bird's beak bears Goya's name. In the scene above, Goya finds a piquant beauty and bearing in *majas*, girls of a questionable social order. Feminine to their fingertips, the girls reflect an air of mystery that is heightened by the man watching from the shadows.

on Manuel Osorio de Zuñiga, detail

From his position at the center of the turbulent Spanish scene, Goya was acutely aware of history and the people, events and institutions that mold it. Early in his career, the office of the Inquisition (and the churchmen who ran it) was the most brutal, powerful and repressive force in all of Spanish society. Its judgments extended to political and social affairs as well as to ecclesiastical matters. Goya's picture *(below)* shows an Inquisition trial scene, the

accused wearing penitential cloth overgarments and tall, cone hats. The despairing defendants are downcast, suspecting their fate is sealed. The clerics sit back smugly to watch the show. A measure of Goya's ability to influence the viewer is found in this painting. Like most creative men of his time, he hated the Inquisition, but he conveys this emotion through the harsh reality of the scene rather than by caricature.

Judicial Session of the Inquisition, detail

II

The Apprentice Years

A limp, life-sized dummy is tossed by four smiling girls in this tapestry cartoon, one of Goya's last, painted late in 1791 or early in 1792. Such play was a familiar diversion at certain Spanish outdoor festivals. But the coquettish air of the girls and the hopelessness of the dummy man may be Goya's way of illustrating the pleasure that some women derive from toying with males, a theme that preoccupied him.

The Dummy, 1791-1792

A persistent legend has the 17-year-old Goya fleeing Saragossa hurriedly and perhaps incognito, either as the result of an unfortunate love affair or because of some trouble with ecclesiastical authorities. Unfortunately, as with so many of the most intriguing tales about Goya's young manhood, there is no reliable evidence to support this story. One of his earlier biographers has suggested, in a much-quoted line, that "if Goya had written an autobiography, it would perhaps be as fascinating as that of the famous Benvenuto Cellini." Yet the same man, who was in a position to gather reminiscences from contemporaries of the young artist, summarizes his friends' opinions of Goya's character as "original, frank, modest, courageous and untroubled"—hardly the Goya of legend. Undoubtedly he had bohemian friends and affected bohemian airs, in the great tradition of student artists. But his prudence, even at this tender age, more than balanced whatever instinct for troublemaking he may have had.

On his arrival in Madrid, Goya applied for a grant from the Royal Academy of San Fernando, the official center of the fine arts in Spain, but in the competition for this treasured prize, which ended January 15, 1764, he received not a single vote. For two years thereafter history records not a single mention of Francisco Goya. It is believed that he stayed on in Madrid, but no one knows where—or if—he studied painting, how he supported himself, who his friends were. It has simply been assumed that he lived in one of the city's poorer quarters, eking out some sort of hand-to-mouth existence, soaking up that knowledge of the common life of his times that is so evident in his later work. But no one knows for certain how he passed the time from a point just prior to his 18th birthday to a date just prior to his 20th.

It is known, however, that at this moment in its history the city of Madrid was undergoing tremendous changes. However Goya lived in the capital, it may be assumed that as a sensitive and intelligent young man he was not unaware of a new, not fully formed, but nonetheless stimulating spirit abroad in the streets. By 1764 Spain had known 16 warless years, first under the reign of the unremarkable but determinedly pacifis-

This contemporary engraving depicts one of the most delightful innovations made in Madrid during a drive to beautify the city that was initiated before Goya arrived there —the installation of a complex of promenades, drives and fountains around the Royal Palace of the Retiro, visible at the right. The popularity of the Avenue of the Prado, as the area is still called, is illustrated in the print. Throngs enjoy an evening stroll, while carriages of the rich sedately circle the tree-shaded drive. Bright with the costumes of *majas, majos* and dandies, ringing with the gay calls of orange and nut venders, the avenue also attracted gangs of rowdy boys who sang ribald songs and stripped to splash in the fountains.

tic Ferdinand VI, who succeeded his father, Philip V. Peace continued under the quite remarkable rule of Ferdinand's half-brother, Charles III, who was perhaps the only genuinely enlightened monarch Spain has ever experienced. Charles was the first son that Philip V had by his second wife, Isabel Farnese, and it was for him that she had so destructively fought and schemed to achieve the kingdom of Naples and Sicily. As if to compensate for the misery his mother had created in Spain, Charles devoted his well-disciplined, tireless energy to a long overdue attempt at broad-scale reform when he ascended the Spanish throne.

"The King has a very odd appearance in person and dress," an English diplomat in Madrid wrote. "He is of diminutive stature, with a complexion the color of mahogany. He has not been measured for a coat these thirty years, so that it sits on him like a sack." But for all his eccentricity of appearance he was, as another English observer put it, a man of "good talents, a happy memory, and uncommon command of himself on all occasions. His having been often deceived renders him suspicious. He ever prefers carrying a point by gentle means, and has the patience to repeat exhortations rather than exert his authority. . . . Yet, with the greatest gentleness, he keeps his ministers and attendants in the utmost awe."

The King had his foibles. He was afflicted by a melancholia that ran in his family (his father had finally been driven mad by it), and there was an austerity about his style of life that somewhat alienated him from the aristocrats of his court and the diplomats posted to it. They would have preferred a less sober social life than he decreed, and his dislike of music and the theater, his absolute abhorrence of the bull ring (he even attempted to ban this most popular of spectacles) puzzled and offended many of his subjects. His only diversion was a passion for the hunt—he spent several methodical hours each day in the field with his gun—which ill suited his essentially gentle nature but provided a blessed relief from the melancholy moods that plagued him.

Charles' quirks, however, were of little consequence when compared to his virtues. The most significant of these were his capacity for hard work, an ability to accept and try new ideas and a resistance to government through court intrigue—qualities rarely exhibited by Spanish

30

sovereigns. In addition, he had a high sense of honor, which was most often exhibited, as it was by many Spaniards, in a fanatical devotion to the principle that his word was his bond—"Spanish probity is proverbial," wrote a contemporary French observer. He was courageous in his convictions, deeply pious and had a great love of family.

Charles' progress during the first seven years of his reign was slow. At the age of 16 he had left Spain for Italy, and he was 43 when he returned, totally unfamiliar with the Spanish scene and spirit. He depended excessively in these early years on advisers he had brought with him from his Neapolitan principality, and they managed to offend a sizable percentage of the population with a number of unwise, if minor, edicts. Nevertheless, his predecessor Ferdinand VI had set in train a number of reforms—reorganizing the navy, abolishing a particularly hated sales tax, subsidizing mines and industries in the hope of making them competitive with their rivals elsewhere in Europe, building roads and canals and even making a start at ending Spain's intellectual isolation by sending students abroad to pursue advanced studies. Moreover, the ideas of the French Enlightenment had begun to take hold in Spain. There was now a Spanish Royal Academy based on the French model, and it was publishing a magazine and had brought out a dictionary in hopes of standardizing the language, one of the traditional first steps in building a sense of national unity. This kind of work continued during the first years of Charles' reign and was the precondition for the Spanish Enlightenment—a truncated, unfulfilled, but enormously stimulating period that would provide the intellectual background against which Goya's first 20 years of professional activity will have to be placed.

During the years before Goya's arrival in Madrid, however, the changes taking place in the city were more physical than spiritual. In particular, the gigantic new Royal Palace, which had been under construction for some 30 years, was nearing completion. This had two salutary effects on the city. In the first place, it was decided that the capital itself would have to be renovated if it was to be worthy of the grand 1,200-room neoclassical building whose designs had been approved by Philip V and Isabel Farnese. Broad avenues were thrust through the old quarters of the city and were, indeed, extended beyond the old city limits. Impressive government buildings were erected along the new boulevards, and Madrid began to assume the look of a modern metropolis. Moreover, the city was provided with street lights, sanitation services, and an improved water supply and a reasonably efficient police force. Spaniards had always had an affection for the communal enjoyment of streets and squares, perhaps because of the bustling contrast to the austerity of their homes. Street fairs, religious processions, performances by strolling jugglers, even the bullfights, which often took place in open plazas in those days, formed one of the distinguishing characteristics of Spanish life. Now, with the city's streets cleaner and safer, this life became more vital than ever in Madrid. The twilight stroll along one of the great avenues—a time for flirtation, argument and pre-prandial relaxation and refreshment—became a custom that persists today. There is no question that Goya himself took a particular delight in the pastime. The sense of teeming, thronging life that pervades so much of his work is clearly derived from an appreciation of his adopted city's street life.

Goya was beginning to find his subject matter. As an aspiring artist, however, he was undoubtedly more interested in the struggle for artistic power that was beginning to be waged in Madrid. This struggle was the second good effect that the completion of the palace had on the life of the city. For years there had been no significant artistic production in Spain. The scene was dominated by a succession of minor French painters—none of whom excited more than passing interest among the Spaniards. But suddenly, at least in court circles, there was a flurry of concern about art. Here was this vast palace, the walls and ceilings of its hundreds of public and private rooms crying out for decoration, and there was no one at hand to do the job, because, as an English traveler of the time noted, "If one hears of an artist, one is sure to find him a foreigner, for the arts have made but little progress amongst the natives."

And so the call for help went out. The first to respond was Anton Raphael Mengs, 33 years old, strong, masterful and certain that he had discovered in the classical style the one true path to beauty. A year later, in 1762, the Venetian Giovanni Battista Tiepolo, accompanied by two sons whose artistic training he had supervised, also appeared in Madrid. Tiepolo was old now, and worn out by a career that had taken him all over Italy and to Germany as well, fulfilling an endless series of decorating commissions. Still, he was undoubtedly the last great master of the Rococo style. And so the two major forces of mid-18th Century art, personified by two of their best-known practitioners, confronted one another in direct competition for a monarch's favor.

Of the two, Tiepolo was incomparably the greater artist. He exuberantly broke all the academic rules of design, the laws of physical motion, even the law of gravity. His colors were wonderfully warm and alive, his crowded compositions marvelously bold and free. He successfully painted religious subjects, but what he truly loved was pagan mythology, sending its thinly veiled gods and goddesses "frolicking through space, chasing one another among the planets or making love on a cushion of clouds." But whether he was painting the saints of Christianity or the deities of Greece and Rome, his real subject was man—graceful, sportive, thoughtless, on the move. Tiepolo's open, dynamic paintings always seemed to want to escape their boundaries, which is perhaps why his best work was done on the spacious walls and ceilings of palaces. No one has ever claimed profundity for Tiepolo's work—only delight. And his painting truly reflected his personality. "He is full of wit and zest, easy to deal with, bubbling over with ideas," a contemporary wrote; "he . . . works at a prodigious speed; he paints a picture in less time than it takes another artist to mix his colors."

Tiepolo was in every way the antithesis of Mengs, whose rather effeminate features belied a stern will and a sober dedication to an artistic ideology that he was convinced—rightly as it turned out—was about to supercede the Rococo as the height of fashion. That style was the neoclassic, and it was not only closer to the spirit of Mengs' age but was, in fact, a product of that spirit. The leading minds of the Enlightenment that was sweeping Europe—in particular the French *philosophes* Voltaire, Rousseau and Diderot—loved classical antiquity. To them, the Golden Age of Greece seemed the first (and possibly the last) great age of reason, and in the achievements of that heroic era they sought an antidote to the forces of unreason, which they felt had dominated European civilization.

Curiously, the chief architect of the revival of the classical spirit in art was not an artist at all but a scholar. In 1764 a German archeologist, Johann Joachim Winckelmann, published a book that was to set the tone for the future. Winckelmann had fallen under the spell of Italy's treasures while excavating ancient sites and doing research in the Vatican collections. He released his findings in his monumental and monumentally influential *History of Ancient Art.* As history, Winckelmann's survey was often inaccurate in detail, but to an audience of intellectuals predisposed to its point of view, it was powerfully persuasive. The most prominent characteristic of classical art, Winckelmann wrote, was "a noble simplicity and silent greatness in pose as well as in expression . . . revealing in the midst of passion a great and steadfast soul." Against this ideal he contrasted the Rococo artists' tendency toward "exaggerated poses and action accompanied by an insolent 'dash' that they regard as spiritedness." Hateful. But Winkelmann was philosophical about it. The modern age was still in its adolescence, it might still aspire to the serenity that the ancient world had achieved in its maturity. "In all human activity the violent and transitory develops first: poise and profundity appear last . . . only great masters have them."

It was a fine theory, but in practice it directed the neoclassic artists away from life and toward a kind of frozen literalism that makes one think that they painted from statues rather than human models. Movement disappeared from their work and with it went the warm flow of color and line that animated the Baroque and Rococo periods. In its place came formal compositions, heroic in conception, but severe, static, lacking the fanciful delights of the more spontaneous, less intellectualized style that was its enemy.

The last, glorious flourish of the Rococo style in Spain can be seen in the brilliant commissions that Charles III entrusted to Tiepolo and his sons. It is their cloud-filled fresco—over 140 square yards of an *Apotheosis of the Spanish Monarchy (page 41)*—that decorates the ceiling of the *saleta* of the Royal Palace in Madrid. And there are several other equally bright and lively Tiepolo works in the throne room and elsewhere in the royal residence. Charles III evidently liked the work of the Tiepolo family well enough, but his judgment was to be badly shaken before long. Tiepolo had painted seven altarpieces for a church near the royal summer residence at Aranjuez after completing his works for the palace. Intense and dramatic, they would have seemed unexceptionable in every way. But the King's confessor, who fancied himself a connoisseur of art and was a friend of Tiepolo's rivals, condemned the pictures as crude, pagan and alien to the spirit of Spain. He had all seven paintings removed from the church and replaced with works by Mengs and two other neoclassicists. Thereafter, although Tiepolo was not entirely cut off from official commissions, his life in Madrid became an empty one. Wearied by his long artistic labors—he was 74—and his fight against the influence of Mengs, Tiepolo died in Madrid in 1770.

Tiepolo lived long enough, however, to see his rival become the greatest power in Spanish art. Mengs had worked hard for his success. He was one of those unfortunate children whose father insisted that he must become first a prodigy and then a master of world stature. The old man —a painter of miniatures—had taken his son from his native Dresden to Rome at the age of 12. He locked the youngster in the Vatican galleries every day, thoughtfully providing him with a bottle of water and a crust of bread to sustain him, and insisted that he copy, copy, copy until he acquired technical facility.

This discipline did wonderous things for Mengs' will, but it appears to have done almost nothing for his imagination. Friendship with Winckelmann and conversion to the doctrines of neoclassicism remedied that defect, however. His new-found ideology gave him a wide range of subjects and the welcome discipline of a style. As he saw it, the neoclassic artist had a moral duty to eliminate the imperfections of the natural world, to paint things not as they were, but as they ideally ought to be.

It was a very rational way to paint a picture, and it appealed to an intellectual community that exalted rationalism above all else. When he arrived in Spain, the 33-year-old Mengs was already a famous painter. To obtain Mengs' services Charles III had had to provide him with a stipend of 2,000 doubloons per year, a house, a coach and free passage to Spain aboard a man-of-war. At that, the King was fortunate to have him —within a few years, Mengs was turning down other royal commissions. So impressed was Charles by Mengs' first works that he appointed him director of the Royal Academy of San Fernando, from which post he reorganized the royal art collections, dispensed patronage and became, in effect, the dictator of Spanish art.

Tiepolo raged against him—in vain. But discretion was imperative for the younger Spanish artists, none of whom had international reputations to fall back on. The majority of them accepted Mengs' ascendancy quietly. And so did Goya. But there can be no doubt that his allegiance at this time was to the Baroque and Rococo—the styles taught him by Luzán, the styles most often to be observed in Spain before Mengs' arrival, and, most important, the styles whose energies surely appealed to his temperament more than the frigidity of neoclassicism ever could.

Nevertheless, Goya did his best to force himself into the new mode. In 1766 his name emerges in the public records again, this time as a candidate in the triennial competition sponsored by the Mengs-directed Royal Academy of San Fernando. The subject set by the Academy's examiners could not have been less suited to Goya's temperament. It was drawn from Spanish history and had to be painted in oil on a canvas six feet wide and four and a half feet high. It was to be "Martha, Empress of Constantinople presents herself to King Alfonso the Wise in Burgos, to ask him for a third of the sum with which she has agreed to ransom her husband, the Emperor Valduino, from the Sultan of Egypt; and the King of Spain commands that she be given the whole sum."

This mouthful of a work was due by July, seven months after the official announcement. In addition, the competitors were required to report to the Academy at 8:30 a.m. on July 22, allow themselves to be shut up in a room for two and a half hours and paint another, "instantaneous" work on a subject kept secret from them until they entered the testing room. The examiners this time set them the task of portraying the moment in history when "Juan de Urbina and Diego de Paredes, in Italy, upon seeing the Spanish army, discuss to which of the two the arms of the Marqués of Pescara should be given." At 11:45 a.m., the nine judges, having quickly examined the work, decided that the first prize—a three ounce gold medal—should go to Ramón Bayeu. It was by no means an odd choice, since Ramón's elder brother Francisco, who had been Luzán's pupil in Saragossa 12 years before Goya, was a member of the jury. Goya received not one vote. He could console himself only with the judges' polite regret at being unable to reward all the competitors since "in the general opinion of the professors, they were all worthy of it."

Goya learned a lesson from this experience. If he was going to succeed within the Academy, he would need some lessons in the neoclassical style. What better model than Francisco Bayeu himself? He was a conscientious draftsman and a technically accomplished painter who, though he lacked fire and originality, had become a highly successful entrepreneur of his own modest talents. There was much to be learned from such a man. Bayeu, who was remembered by his contemporaries as being both surly in manner and kindly in spirit, seems to have agreed to take on Goya as an assistant. Apparently they got along, for the young artist stayed at least three years—long enough to form an attachment for Bayeu's younger sister, Josefa, whom he would later marry.

Happy as he may have been in this period, Goya evidently felt a certain restlessness. There was something in him that could not find expression in Bayeu's studio. At about the age of 23, he decided he must try to discover what it was and how he might bring it forth. And so, not unmindful of its possibilities for adventure as well as its possibilities for broadening his artistic vision, he decided to make a journey to Italy.

Mystery surrounds Goya's trip. Estimates of the length of his stay in Italy range from a few months to a few years—the most reasonable guess is about two years including time spent in travel. Legend is that he worked his way across Spain as a matador, an interesting but questionable notion. It is a possibility, however, since it was not unusual for a penniless young man in those days to attach himself to a bullfighter's *cuadrilla* to earn money for expenses and to feel the safety of numbers in such an entourage—which could be very comforting on the bandit-plagued Spanish roads. Further support for this irresistibly romantic notion of Goya as bullfighter is lent by two letters: in one, Goya jokingly signs himself "Francisco de los Toros"; in another, a friend reveals that in his eightieth year, Goya reminisced that "he fought bulls in his time, and that with his sword in hand he feared no one." Some credence may have to be given to Goya's boasts, since this is the period when least is known about him. He was the right age for the profession he later claimed, and it is the only time when a career in the bull ring can be fitted into his biography. Nevertheless, while Goya, like most provincial

In 1795 Goya was putting the final touches to this portrait of his brother-in-law and mentor, Francisco Bayeu, when his subject died at the age of 61. Although Goya's relationship with Francisco vacillated between friendship and antagonism, he remained friendly all his life with a younger Bayeu, Manuel, who was also a painter.

boys, probably jumped into a bull ring at one time or another, a more conservative conjecture as to how he made his way to Italy is in order. Probably lacking the money to book passage by sea, it is likely that he traveled overland, earning his keep by seeking such minor artistic jobs as he could find en route. The evidence of his later life, when a modest acquaintance with the French language appears, suggests that Goya moved at a leisurely pace through France, pausing long enough to begin learning French and to copy a few paintings before moving on to Rome.

A good many legends surround Goya's Roman holiday. The most innocuous has him occasionally supporting himself as a street acrobat. Another finds him briefly tempted by an offer from the Russian ambassador to go to St. Petersburg to work as a court painter. He was said to have climbed the dome of St. Peter's to inscribe his initials at the highest point ever achieved there by a writer of graffiti. And he was reported to have fallen so deeply in love with a nun that he attempted to raid her convent to carry her off. It is claimed that only the intervention of the Spanish ambassador saved him—possibly from the gallows. The source of these stories was the small colony of Spanish artists then residing in Italy. But most of the legends were dredged by Goya's early biographers out of old men's memories years after the fact.

The question of which—if any—of these stories is true is, in the last analysis, an insignificant one. The important thing about Goya's sojourn abroad is that it opened his eyes and his mind to the infinite possibilities of his art. He probably went equipped with letters of introduction and used them. He most likely met Mengs, who had returned to Italy briefly to recover his health; and he may have seen Tiepolo's son, Domenico, and from him obtained letters that opened the doors of homes and palaces decorated by the old master; he perhaps contacted Don José Nicolás de Azara, a fellow Aragonese and an official at the Vatican, who would have helped him to gain access to other private art collections.

What impressed him the most? He left no records, only the merest traces of influence in his own work, and these are difficult to discern. Surely, in Rome, he saw the work of Michelangelo and Raphael on the walls and ceilings of the Vatican. But his reaction to these giants, if any, is lost. Only the brilliant frescoes at Parma by the 16th Century master Correggio find an echo in Goya's own fresco decorations made later for a church in Madrid. Among his artistic contemporaries, Goya certainly knew Piranesi's dark, grim prison scenes—appreciating them as much for their fantastical qualities as for their remarkable draftsmanship. He also probably knew the work of Alessandro Magnasco, whose renderings of the follies of ecclesiastics prefigure Goya's own later studies of man's inhumanity to man. And, on the lighter side, he undoubtedly came in contact with the delightful drawing-room scenes of the Venetian Pietro Longhi and the newly popular pictures of the common people and their life in the streets by such artists as Giuseppe Maria Crespi and Giacomo Ceruti. All of these influences, if they can be called that, worked on Goya's mind largely by implication, encouraging him not so much to try these ways as to find his own. And none of them had such immediate impact on him as his immersion in the Italian Baroque and Rococo.

Living in daily contact with the florid Italian styles, absorbing them at first hand and at their best rather than through prints and the instruction of second-rate teachers, Goya committed himself fully. In the process, he ended his struggle to accept the discipline of academic neoclassicism as exemplified by Mengs. The Baroque and Rococo were not, of course, perfectly suited to him, but at least they were alive and moved.

Late in his stay in Italy, Goya was attracted by the announcement of a painting competition being held by the Academy of Fine Arts at Parma, in the north. What better way to return to Spain—to crown his Italian adventure—than as the winner of an academic contest? The announced theme was "Hannibal sights Italy on crossing the Alps." But the rules stipulated that foreign artists must submit their works to an Academy delegate in the town where they were living. Goya, far from home, resorted to a minor subterfuge. Signing his name "Goja," in the Italian fashion, he declared himself a "Romano" or Roman and a pupil of "Vajeu" (Francisco Bayeu), painter to the King of Spain. This may have permitted him to send his picture directly to Parma, thus avoiding possible rejection before his picture reached the final judges. In any case, Goya's entry received six votes, more than any competitor except one. Paolo Borroni—whose name is practically unknown in art save for this brief contact with Goya—carried off the only prize, a five ounce gold medal. Goya had to console himself with flattering mentions in the jury's report, which stated that if he had been more truthful to nature in his coloring and less eccentric in composing the subject he would have won. Possibly disheartened by his defeat and probably disenchanted with the life of an *émigré*, Goya made plans to return to Spain. He made his way home as he had arrived—by unknown means.

At this point in his life, the 25-year-old Goya had a reasonably mature complement of technical skills, but he still did not have a style that was truly his own. He clearly wished to move beyond the Baroque and Rococo styles he had known so well in Italy. Neoclassicism was, for him, a dead end. Even if he had possessed a personal vision at this time, it is doubtful that he was psychologically ready to express it. One of his more recent biographers, José Gudiol, rejecting the conventionalized romance of Goya's legend, describes him as "a timid man, governed by emotion and somewhat lacking in self-confidence." It is a sound judgment, especially in relation to Goya's management of his own career at this stage of life, and it is borne out particularly by the artist's decision to begin his professional life on congenial home ground in Saragossa, rather than in the fiercely competitive atmosphere of Madrid.

It must always be remembered that Goya was, and remained, a provincial at heart. Although he lusted after the pleasures of the sophisticated world of fashion and ideas, he never felt truly at ease in that world. Rather, he seems to have felt that he would conquer it only if his art was strong enough to compensate for his defects of personal manner. This would account for the appeal of Saragossa at this stage of his career. It was a familiar and undemanding place where he could concentrate on his work, free of the pressures he would surely have felt in Madrid. Here he could gain confidence in his abilities, and when he was ready to approach Madrid again he could do so with a string of successes behind him and perhaps even some capital to finance his establishment.

The plan succeeded. Goya arrived in Saragossa in June 1771, and by late summer he had his first important commission—a series of wall paintings for a chapel in the Sobradiel Palace owned by the Counts of Gabarda. There are three large works in this group—all depicting episodes from the Bible and all copied from French and Italian engravings. Goya showed somewhat more originality in painting four smaller figures of saints. All seven, however, are fairly conventional religious works, showing a certain joyousness of spirit and technique but little else of a striking nature.

Goya's work apparently pleased his patrons well enough. Indeed, word of his success probably got around, for in October he was asked by the building committee of the Shrine of Our Lady of the Pillar in Saragossa to submit sketches for a fresco they wished to commission for a cupola. Within three weeks Goya delivered a sketch of his design. The committee was pleased. They were even more pleased when they learned that Goya's price for the work would be 10,000 reales less than his nearest competitor's. Having presented a picture painted in fresco to prove his ability in the technique of the final work, Goya was asked by the committee to prepare yet another provisional sketch, which they insisted upon submitting to the Royal Academy of San Fernando in Madrid for approval. Apparently the provincial churchmen did not trust their own judgment of the work of a comparatively untried artist.

When Goya submitted his sketch, in January 1772, the committee was so delighted with it that they decided to accept it immediately, without consulting the Academicians in Madrid. By the end of June, Goya had completed the painting, which was entitled *The Adoration of the Name of God,* and received the last third of his fee of 15,000 reales (about $3,750). The fresco is almost pure Baroque—choirs of angels, predominantly female figures, disport themselves on billows of clouds, while above hovers a golden triangle bathed in light representing the Trinity and inscribed in Hebrew with the Name of God. The popularity of the work established Goya as Aragon's leading artist.

Within three years, the tax rolls—still one of the only sources of documentation of Goya's life—reveal that he was Saragossa's most prosperous painter, even surpassing in this respect both his former teacher, Luzán and Juan Andrés Mercklein, the dean of the area's artists. Many of the smaller works Goya did in this period, portraits of leading citizens and minor nobility, have been lost, but among those that remain are paintings of the Fathers of the Church for a chapel in the city of Muel. Frugal with his ideas, he repeated the same paintings—this time on canvas rather than plaster—for the parish church of Remolinos. These works show a certain fluidity and freedom in their execution, indicating that Goya was at last beginning to gain the self-confidence he needed.

He was even beginning to take his first tentative steps away from the conventions of the Baroque style. The other major work of his Saragossa period, 11 large frescoes for the walls of the church of the Carthusian Monastery of Aula Dei, are ravaged now by time, weather and war, and they bear witness to an artist struggling to finish a large task as quickly as possible. But these renderings of tales from the Gospel are far more austere than any of the known works that precede them. They are dominated by awesomely tall figures; their composition is determinedly simple and the brushstrokes suggest effects without laboring over them. Here Goya has abandoned the flights of angels, the glimpses of celestial glory that were so characteristic of Baroque church decoration and that he had employed in his earlier work. For the first time, the Goya that was to come shows his hand.

His career in general, and the work on the monastery frescoes in particular, was going so well that, in the spring of 1773, Goya broke off his labors at Aula Dei and traveled to Madrid to claim the hand in marriage of Josefa Bayeu, the sister of his former teacher. He could afford a bride now. Furthermore, he must have felt that it would not hurt his career to attach his name more closely to that of Bayeu, who was by this time the most prominent Spanish painter. Whatever Goya's motives for marrying —passionate love does not seem prominent among them—he appears to have encountered no opposition from Bayeu himself. In May 1773 the older artist applied to the King (he was a court painter) for a raise in salary on the grounds that one of his sisters was about to marry. On July 25, the ceremony took place, and Josefa entered what has rightly been called "the dense shadow in which she was destined to live by the side of her husband." Their marriage lasted for 39 years, until her death in 1812. Of the children she bore Goya—the number is unknown—only one survived to maturity. Beyond that, however, nothing is known of Josefa. She apparently took little interest in her husband's work or in the life of the society around her. Goya is known to have painted her only once—the portrait *(page 48)* reveals a slender, thin-lipped woman with large eyes, even features and reddish-blonde hair. By the time her husband got around to painting Josefa, time and cares had etched her face with fine lines, and there is a distance, an emptiness, in her expression that many take to be the measure of the distance and the emptiness that existed in her marriage. She functioned not as an inspiration to Goya but as a balancing force in his emotional life. Whatever the fluctuations of his fortunes or his moods, she kept his household running smoothly and quietly. History records not a single remark by or about Josefa Goya. She was simply there when and if Goya needed her.

Josefa returned to Saragossa with Goya while he finished work on the Aula Dei frescoes. And then, late in 1774, Goya received the call for which he had been waiting. Mengs had returned to Madrid to undertake, among other assignments for the crown, the artistic reform of the Royal Tapestry Manufactory of Santa Barbara in Madrid. Francisco Bayeu was to assist him in this enterprise and was in a position to handle most of the patronage connected with it. And so Goya and several other artists of his generation—among them, not surprisingly, Ramón Bayeu —were engaged to create the cartoons on which the weavers would base their work. The job promised to be steady and remunerative—the perfect base on which to build a career in Madrid. Most important, Goya felt himself ready for the assignment.

Madrid's Art Establishment

When the 18-year-old Goya first arrived in Madrid in 1764, he discovered a city whose artistic life was polarized between two opposing forces, the neoclassical and the Rococo, led respectively by a young German, Anton Raphael Mengs, and Giovanni Battista Tiepolo, an aging Venetian. Both had journeyed to Spain at the invitation of Charles III to help decorate the vast walls and ceilings of his glorious, newly completed Royal Palace. Inheritor of the dramatic Baroque style that had swept Europe in the previous century, Tiepolo had refined that tradition into one of billowing, colorful eloquence in such frescoes as the one he threw across the ceiling of an antechamber to the throne room *(right)*. Pulsing with pageantry, glowing with light and filled with movement, this magnificent fresco was among the last of Tiepolo's large-scale decorations. Mengs, on the other hand, brought to Spain the new, cool, rational spirit of neoclassic painters who sought the harmony, calm and grandeur of ancient Greece and Rome.

Goya and his fellow Spaniards were to choose between these styles in different ways. Some, like Luis Meléndez, turned to neoclassism. Others—Goya's brother-in-law Francisco Bayeu among them—loosely adapted both styles. At first Goya did the same, but with an instinct for tough-minded realism and an adroit blending of elements he discovered in the art of Spain's past, he forged his own approach to painting.

A soaring panorama of allegorical figures pays homage to Spain, represented by the glorious woman enthroned high in the center. At the upper left, two winged cupids accompany Mercury, who bears a crown. At the lower right, Mars, clad in armor, and Venus, clutching Eros, approach in grandeur.

Tiepolo: *Apotheosis of the Spanish Monarchy*, fresco detail, 1764-1766

Anton Raphael Mengs: *Charles III*, 1761

Two portraits of King Charles III illustrate striking differences between the neoclassical style of Mengs and the more realistic approach that Goya later developed. Every detail of Mengs' idealized likeness at the left calls attention to Charles' station: the jewel-encrusted Maltese Cross hanging from his neck, his stately posture and splendid suit of armor—all point to kingship. Goya's portrait is admittedly more informal and contains only

Charles III, c.1780

passing reference to the King's rank—the silk sash and medal on his chest. Goya evoked the personality of the man himself. An enthusiastic hunter, Charles is depicted in the field with musket and hound, wearing informal clothes and a rakish tricorn hat. These details, together with his relaxed posture and the twinkle in his eye, have a humanizing effect and suggest a king whose personality was both warm and gently charming.

43

Francisco Bayeu: *Picnic in the Country*, c.1780

Picnic on the Banks of the Manzanares, 1776

Among the important native painters during Goya's early years in Madrid were Luis Meléndez and Francisco Bayeu. A popular and successful painter of still lifes, Meléndez depicted himself *(right)* proudly displaying a drawing of a statuesque male nude—a mark of his Academic background. Cool, smooth and unpenetrating, Meléndez's portrait is typical of the superficial style that Goya's strongly emotional work would supplant.

Francisco Bayeu, whose sister Goya married, was a help in the younger painter's career, but of limited artistic influence. This can be seen in the paintings above, designs for tapestries that both artists prepared for the Royal Tapestry Manufactory. Bayeu's scene, although only a sketch, is stiff and formal; Goya's is fluid and natural.

Luis Meléndez: *Self-Portrait*, c.1780

45

Rembrandt van Rijn: *The Raising of Lazarus,* 1632

Goya is reported to have once said that among his "masters" were Rembrandt and Velázquez. If so, he must have been attracted by Rembrandt prints like the one above, in which Christ raises Lazarus from the dead in a burst of light that shatters the darkness of a tomb. Indeed, Goya would eventually use such effects of light and dark (chiaroscuro) not only in his own graphic works, but also in a magnificent series of canvases known as his "Black Paintings" *(pages 173-185).*

Velázquez was a nearer inspiration. In 1778 Goya had begun a series of etchings of the master's works as

illustrations for a book. Among them, of course, was *Las Meninas (above, at right)* in which Velázquez shows himself *(left)* painting the King and Queen, who are reflected in a mirror, while Princess Margarita looks on with her dwarf, her dog and her retinue. Goya's copy is something less than exact, but his own later works show how much he absorbed from Velázquez. The sharp sense of psychological reality in his portraits, the solid, yet unstudied composition, the easy handling of details of dress and setting—all these things, plus a sense of life beneath the surface, emerge as parts of Goya's greatness.

Diego Velázquez: *Las Meninas*, 1656

Las Meninas after Velázquez, 1778

III

Making It
in Madrid

The Madrid to which Goya returned with his bride in 1774 was, in its way, as different from the city he had left five years before as Goya now was from the student he had been. The physical renovation of the capital had proceeded apace, but the most important change had been one of atmosphere. In 1766, at precisely the time Goya was at work on his ill-fated competition picture for the Academy, Charles III, acceding to some singularly bad advice from the courtiers who had accompanied him from Naples, published a decree prohibiting Spanish men from wearing their traditional costume—a flowing cape and slouch hat. These clothes, it was argued, provided criminals with an easy disguise and thus hindered police work. Accordingly, backed by a police escort, tailors were stationed in doorways around the city where, equipped with large shears, they summarily executed the order.

It was, seemingly, a small matter, especially in contrast to the kind of unwise regulation Spaniards were used to accepting with passive indifference. It proved, however, to be an intrusion on a most basic form of self-expression, an attack on a point of personal pride that to an 18th Century Spaniard was intolerable. For 10 days the Madrileños rioted, stoning the houses of ministers, even attacking the guards of the Royal Palace. The King was forced to rescind his order. More important, Charles decided to rid himself of his foreign advisers and replace them with Spaniards. In so doing, he drew together at his court, in positions of genuine power, men who could focus and direct the forces of reform that had been stirring in his country for a quarter of a century.

The first of these men was the Count of Aranda, a clever, irritatingly self-assured aristocrat who nourished a dream of yanking his nation out of its centuries-old torpor and, in a single generation, propelling it to the forefront of the Enlightenment. He solved the cape-and-hat problem neatly enough by declaring them the official uniform of the hangman. Since no one wanted to be mistaken for that gentleman, the costume quickly disappeared from the streets. Aranda had other successes, too—in currency reform and in beginning a secular, state-supported school system. But he overreached himself. In one swift, cruel stroke he ordered the entire Jesuit order—some 10,000 priests—to leave Spain and its colonies. He also curbed the powers of the Inquisition, forcing it to confine itself to questions of heresy and apostasy and ending its activities in secular affairs. Neither move was popular in Spain, and by the time Goya returned to Madrid the King had appointed Aranda ambassador to France—where he was to find the atmosphere far more congenial.

Following Aranda's removal, although Charles retained an Italian as Prime Minister, he turned to more moderate but hardly less enlightened men for counsel. Among them were the Count of Floridablanca, Pedro de Campomanes and Gaspar Melchor de Jovellanos, an economist, poet and reformer who was subsequently to earn the title of "the most eminent Spaniard of his age." Over the next two decades, no portion of the Spanish economy was untouched by the reforms these men set in train. They ended the monopoly Seville and Cádiz had enjoyed in trading with the New World and extended the benefits of that trade to other ports. Under their influence, royal edicts encouraged the formation of large-scaled private industry and attempted to remove the traditional stigma attached to manual labor by declaring that craft occupations were compatible with noble rank and that craftsmen would, in future, be eligible for government posts. Ultimately, the new men around the King would even establish a national bank—the Banco Nacional de San Carlos.

The new men were particularly excited by the possibilities of agricultural reform. They sharply curtailed the privileges of the *Mesta*, the centuries-old sheep monopoly. They also did everything in their power to break up the great estates, and they used government assets to create low interest loan funds for the benefit of small farmers. They even encouraged colonizers from Germany and France to settle in the most barren sections of the country where, with government aid, they worked at creating model farming communities. A measure of the widespread interest in such things, even in fashionable society, is that the amorous Italian rogue, Casanova, promoted a job for himself while at a Madrid dinner party in 1768 by pretending some knowledge of the plan to populate the Sierra Morena with Swiss farmers.

Income levels rose fairly steadily throughout Charles' reign, and so did the birth rate—a sign of rising confidence. Yet even with persuasive evidence of its effectiveness, reform did not really capture the mass imagination. Though different in motive and practice, it still looked superficially like more government interference in the people's lives—interference that the Spaniard traditionally detested and that, in this case, was especially abhorrent since the King was considered a foreigner. And there was agonizing difficulty in translating plans into action as they filtered through the huge, inert government bureaucracy and then down to the local level, where resistance to the central government was a natural mode of existence. The new spirit, so evident in Madrid, was therefore unable to root itself very strongly in the Spanish earth. Shortly after Charles III died in 1788, the reforming spirit simply vanished. It was, as one Spaniard wrote, "a flash of lightning illuminating us for one moment only, to leave us in greater darkness."

In Madrid in 1775, however, the light of reason seemed not a mo-

An edict of 1766, outlawing the long cloaks and drooping hatbrims then enormously popular in Madrid, aroused tremendous opposition. Scenes of aroused Madrileños clutching their traditional costume were common as the properly attired constables tried to enforce the edict. A century later, the event was still fresh enough in memory to be the subject of this lithograph, used in a history of the city.

mentary flash but the ray of a steady, rising sun. And that light illuminated a scene of unprecedented activity in court circles. The Spanish Enlightenment may in fact have been "second-rate and derivative" as an intellectual movement, but enthusiasm for the ideas being imported —mainly from France—was none the less for that, and Goya was quickly caught up in it.

Indeed, the influence of the movement on his sensibility and on his subsequent career is incalculable. The leading figures of the Spanish Enlightenment became his friends, patrons and intellectual mentors. In their *tertulias* (salons) he was to gain what he had not gained anywhere else in the course of his wandering, patternless education—an intellectual underpinning for his art. Until now he had been a painter developing the skills of his hand, the sight of his eye. Now he found an ideology, a faith, that gave him a new and more purposeful direction. In Madrid he learned that the basic assumption of the Enlightenment was that what was natural was right, morally and esthetically; that it was the business of intellectuals and artists to explore and define nature with a new precision; that the basic tool they possessed for this great task was their reason. And so he became a disciple of this new, secular religion. It drove him on his expedition to the outermost limits of the human mind, whose darkest regions he mapped with his brush and pencil, and, when the Age of Reason collapsed into an Age of Revolution, he was driven to despair. The artist of the *Caprichos (pages 109-115), The Disasters of War (pages 137-143),* the "Black Paintings" *(pages 173-185)* loathed the bitter truths he felt compelled to commit to paper and canvas. He wrote, for example, that the purpose of the *Caprichos,* his series of etchings that satirize social behavior, was "to banish harmful, vulgar beliefs, and to perpetuate . . . the solid testimony of truth."

The Spanish Enlightenment is an essential perspective from which to view the works of Goya, but at the beginning his involvement with it was quite humble, lying mainly in mild gratitude and a desire to please. On the practical level, he would not have had some important early commissions if the leaders of the Enlightenment had not extended their interest in industrial reform to the arts and crafts. Following the earlier example of France under Louis XIV, they had, over the course of 20 years, established several factories devoted to the manufacture of fine silver, glass and cabinetry, hats and textiles—for a while, the Valencian silk industry matched and even surpassed the excellence of the French weavers. They also encouraged the refurbishing of several other factories, among which was one that would be especially important to Goya—the Royal Tapestry Manufactory. Created by Philip V to compensate for the loss of tapestries that had flowed from Flanders before that country was lost to Spain as a result of war, the Royal Tapestry Manufactory had failed to match expectations. It had fallen far short of the glorious productivity of Paris' Manufacture des Gobelins, which the French Bourbon monarchs had so long subsidized. Spanish work in tapestry largely imitated that of its older rivals in technique and subject matter. However, when the painter Mengs took over as director, he and his assistant Francisco Bayeu, along with their fellow artists, decided to abandon the

In this lithograph made from Goya's portrait of his friend and patron Gaspar Melchor de Jovellanos, the statesman-writer is shown as Minister of Justice, the office he held in 1798. Philosopher, poet, economist and playwright, the many-sided jurist was also a connoisseur of art who valued Goya's friendship. Both a liberal reformer and a patriotic Spaniard, Jovellanos bitterly antagonized Spanish reactionaries, who twice exiled him from Madrid, then imprisoned him in 1801. After his release in 1808, he joined the junta of Cádiz, defiantly refusing to collaborate with the "enlightened" French.

Biblical and mythological themes that had predominated in Spain and elsewhere and to produce compositions based on the realities and pleasantries of country life. This decision was not, of course, in keeping with Mengs' personal esthetic of neoclassicism, but King Charles was beginning to show a predilection for this kind of thing, and his wishes were their commands. Furthermore, the artistic tastes of the Enlightenment justified a trend toward observing ordinary people engaged in ordinary pursuits, animated by an optimistic delight in the foibles and amusements of such folk.

The artists engaged at the Royal Tapestry Manufactory by Mengs and Bayeu had plenty of examples to inspire them. The works of the French genre painters who had tarried briefly at the Spanish court earlier in the century were surely consulted, as were some of the newer French artists. Then, too, the great Tiepolo's son, Lorenzo, had recently completed a series of pastel paintings, which featured various common Madrid types. Thus, in addition to the new dictates of fashion, the young artists had ample precedent before them as they set about making their designs. Goya and Bayeu's younger brother, Ramón, were among the group that was hired.

Goya's first cartoons, as the artist's painted designs for the weavers are called, were hardly masterful. He was assigned a series of hunting and fishing scenes and, although he was something of an outdoorsman, his handling of the material was stiff and reticent. (Always excepting his beloved bulls, Goya was never very skillful with animals.) And he was profoundly uninterested in landscape, perhaps because he was so deeply preoccupied with the human enigma and thus bored by the inanimate details of its setting. It is also likely that he was at least somewhat chastened by the honor and responsibility of undertaking his first royal commission. His developing artistic personality as well as his natural fluency may also have been checked by his need to please his fundamentally antithetical masters, Mengs and Bayeu.

If posterity has given low marks to Goya's first efforts at tapestry design, they pleased his mentors well enough; more commissions were immediately granted him, and they had a salutary effect on his confidence. He turned with quick relief to portrayals of those colorful characters of the lower classes, the *majos*, and their female companions the *majas*. Risen from the pool of impoverished provincials who haunted Madrid's slums, the *majos* were the fashionable toughs who managed to set themselves above their neighbors, and, indeed, in their attitude and bearing, above all Madrid society. Dressed in tight knee-breeches and stockings, shod in buckled low-cut shoes and sporting a vest, a short jacket and large sash—in which they concealed a folding knife called a *navaja* —the *majo* arrogantly strutted down the center of the street, wrapped in a long cape and puffing ostentatiously on a large, black cigar. They had poise and dignity, as did their women, the *majas*—a name that may be drawn from the older word *maya*, meaning queen of the May Day festival. Traditionally, the *maya* was chosen as the most beautiful girl of a district, but by Goya's day, the term *maja* had been extended to all those smartly dressed young women who so enlivened Madrid's street life.

A lady of fashion during Goya's time would not dream of being seen without a fan. Typically, she had dozens, which varied in size and decoration to match her moods and the colors of her dresses. Queen Isabel, the wife of King Philip V, owned 1,626 fans. The fanciest fans were made of expensive, elaborately decorated materials. The ribs of the one above are ivory; the satin webbing bears a painted scene of well-to-do people at a bullfight. The primary purpose of a fan was not to cool a maiden's face, but to communicate her feelings. A tap, for example, could attract a suitor's eyes; a slow lowering was a rebuff, while repeatedly snapping it open and shut might indicate impatience or eager willingness.

The relationship between *majo* and *maja* was ritualistically stormy. Her desire, presumably, was marriage; his was to keep her faithful without resorting to such a disastrous expedient. Inevitably, their encounters exploded into a series of spats, often in public and usually descending quite quickly to physical violence—a result that more often than not ended bloodily because of the *maja's* habit of carrying a poniard held by a garter concealed beneath her skirt.

The open amorality of the lives of the *majos* and *majas,* not to mention their songs and the haunting measures of their dances—the men often played tambourines, castanets and guitars—was extremely appealing to the nobility. Indeed, it was not at all uncommon for the upper classes to find their mistresses and lovers among this group who outwardly so despised their aristocratic airs. By the time Goya began to paint them, majaism had become a fad in society's higher levels.

It has been observed that majaism was the Spanish equivalent of the attraction that the French court under Madame de Pompadour had developed for the style of shepherds and shepherdesses. In France, the nobility's pastoral frolics in the costumes of "Bopeep" and the minor pantheon of mythological divinities are recorded in the frothy, sugar-coated confections of the leading painters of the time, François Boucher and Jean Honoré Fragonard. In Spain, not only the painters, but at least one playwright had taken the characters of the streets for his heroes and heroines. Little playlets based on the boisterous, eventful lives of *majas* and *majos* by Ramón de la Cruz were inserted between the acts of longer works and had become the most popular theatrical attractions in Madrid. Indeed, they were so popular that after the second intermission, when there was no possibility of seeing another skit, the theatres were often deserted. In majaism, Goya found a subject that suited him, suited his audience and suited the deep need of the time—by no means confined to Spain—to get in touch again with the spirit of the people.

In 1777 Goya completed the first group of his memorable tapestry cartoons, among which is *The Parasol*—brilliantly colored, ravishingly painted and yet, somehow, more than an innocent decoration. Simplicity itself, the picture shows a smiling, bright-eyed young girl seated on the ground with her skirt and cloak billowed about her. She holds a folded fan in one hand and supports an adorable black and white pup on her lap. With her is a sturdy young *majo,* attentive and obviously ravished by her beauty, who shields her face from the bright sun with a brilliant green parasol. Suggestions of a stone wall to one side, a wind-whipped tree and leafy glade to the other, do nothing to distract from the two figures. Goya's people are amusing—the coquettish smile and directness of the girl as she gazes, it seems, into the very eyes of the viewer bring forth a smile from any man. Yet they are real in a way that the subjects of Goya's predecessors and competitors in this vein are not. There is, as a critic says, "a positive pinch of earthy actuality"—and an avoidance of sentimentality—that is quite unique and that is to grow in importance as Goya works for the Royal Tapestry Manufactory.

Eventually Goya was to do no less than 63 cartoons, and it is fascinating to watch his development in them. The sunny mood of *The Parasol*

This detail from Goya's *Maja and the Muffled Majos,* painted in 1777, is from a group of tapestry cartoons, which were based on scenes of Madrid's daily life. Here, he has caught his colorfully dressed subjects in characteristic attitudes. The *majas'* saucy charm and quick wit served them well, for they earned a living as street venders, peddling oranges, roasted chestnuts, picnic fare or fripperies, according to the season. Proud of their strength and masculine skills, the *majos* were smiths, butchers, tanners, innkeepers and, on occasion, smugglers.

extends to the group he delivered early in 1778, in which he depicts kite-flying, a game of cards, children playing with a balloon or picking fruit. Shortly thereafter, however, illness intruded upon him, and for several months he felt unable to undertake work on the scale of the tapestry cartoons. Instead, he turned to etching, a technique that he had probably learned earlier. He set about the task of copying 16 of Velázquez' paintings in the royal collections. As copies they were not successful—Goya could not help but try his own variations on the master's work—but the careful study he made of the originals had a profound effect on him. Until this moment he had inexplicably paid little attention to this greatest of Spanish masters. He undoubtedly knew Velázquez, but never before had he confronted him so directly. Now he perceived in Velázquez' work a native tradition far greater, and far better suited to his own temperament than anything in the contemporary styles. Moreover, he saw that Velázquez was a painter who had, a century earlier, practiced what the Enlightenment was now preaching—the close scrutiny of nature, in particular human nature—and that he had a psychological awareness that none of Goya's contemporaries approached.

Goya labored far longer over his copying than the job required. In the process, almost incidentally, he developed the technical skills that were to make him one of the greatest graphic artists the world has ever known. When he returned to the tapestry cartoons, a new spirit began to invade them. At first his subjects were as light-hearted as ever—children and adults still preoccupied by games. But by 1779, less fashionable people, less sportive subjects were introduced. He was still seven years away from such somber work as *The Poor Family at the Well* and *Winter*, an icy study of peasants wrapped in rags, gathering firewood. And he had yet to paint *The Wounded Mason*, a key picture in his development, since it is his first representation of outright tragedy—a workman has fallen from a scaffolding and is either fatally injured or so incapacitated that he will be unable to take up his tools for a long time to come, if ever. But now, in 1779 and 1780, he was, perhaps without being aware of it himself, heading toward these paintings and much else besides.

It is customary for critics to regard the tapestry cartoons as little more than exercises that occasionally hint at things to come. And it is true that in contrast to the powerful work of his late maturity they seem minor. Yet they stand up very well when compared, for example, to the sentimental eroticism with which someone like the Frenchman Fragonard approaches similar material. The case of Goya's tapestry cartoons has been very well put by the modern British critic Michael Levey, who notes that their effectiveness depends on a "power of observation which retains its power by an apparent naïveté. Goya goes on gazing when everyone else has lowered their eyes, seeing everything for the first time. It is candor of vision that was to prove more devastating than any amount of emotional fervor . . . a quality that is akin to the grave scrutiny to which Velázquez subjected his sitters."

Goya continued painting tapestry cartoons off and on until 1792, and they formed the basis of his growing prosperity and celebrity. As early as 1779 he met the King, the Crown Prince and his wife, and he wrote

Zapater: "It fell to me to show them four paintings, and I kissed their hands, and have never been so fortunate in all my life." In the same letter, however, he wrote that "I begin to have greater enemies with greater ill-will." This was to be the pattern of his life for the next decade—a career trending satisfactorily upward, but marked by disappointments, delays and frustrations that depressed and angered him. The time can, perhaps, be seen as one of tempering—the heat of success being cooled by icy plunges into failure. He emerged from it as steel emerges from the same process, toughened and flexible.

Goya's joy at his reception by the Royal Family, for example, turned quickly to gloom a few months later when he applied for a post as one of the Painters to the King and was turned down. A letter from the King's minister, the Duke of Losada, to Don Manuel de Roda, an Aragonese who had pressed Goya's petition, declared that the artist "turns out to be an industrious practitioner of a talent and spirit that promise great advances in his art." "Yet," he added, "there not being any great urgency nor any notable dearth of painters to execute the works offered for royal service, it seems to me that [he] could continue with the paintings for the Tapestry Manufactory, endeavoring in them to do his best to affirm his great proficiency and skill."

A year later, however, Goya managed a success that somewhat compensated for his failure to become Painter to the King—he was elected a Fellow of the Royal Academy of San Fernando. He did so by very deliberately painting a picture that he knew would please. He borrowed from Francisco Bayeu a study for a Crucifixion—which was itself copied from a Mengs—gathered some more ideas from a nude sketch by Bayeu and then prepared a *Christ on the Cross* to accompany his petition for membership. The painting was not so much influenced by his brother-in-law as copied from him. Somber and quietly gleaming, it is nothing at all like his tapestry cartoons—but it served its purpose admirably. On May 7, 1780 he was admitted to the Academy without a single dissenting vote.

That summer a son—"a very beautiful boy"—was born to him, and Goya was once again full of joy. Even the austerity of his life did not rankle. Regarding an impending visit to Saragossa, he wrote Zapater, "I do not need much furniture for my house, since it seems to me that with a print of *Our Lady of the Pillar,* a table, five chairs, a frying-pan, a wine-bag and a small guitar, a roasting spit and an oil lamp, everything else is superfluous." Content though he was with material modesty—at least for a time—his new stature as an Academician confirmed a new resolution in him. Henceforth he would be his own man, less servile to people like Bayeu and to fashion in general than he had been up to now. And just at this moment he was presented with an excellent opportunity to prove his new independence of spirit.

Just after Goya's acceptance in the Academy, Bayeu picked up negotiations that he had conducted earlier for a series of frescoes in the cathedral at Saragossa. There were three domes to be decorated along with some other wall surfaces. Bayeu had completed one of the domes some six years earlier, when he had also arranged that his brother Ramón and Goya were to assist him. Now, Bayeu submitted sketches by the

In 1780 Goya painted the study above as part of his contribution to a huge project for decorating Saragossa's Cathedral of the Pillar. The commission for a series of frescoes, earned by Francisco Bayeu, Goya's brother-in-law, was to be executed by Goya, Francisco Bayeu and his younger brother Ramon. The half-dome painting above, which was designed to complement another by Goya that depicted Mary as Queen of Martyrs, shows angels and a host of saints, among them the beheaded John the Baptist, and Sebastian, pierced by arrows.

younger painters to the cathedral's Council of Works. They were received with "much attention and pleasure," and by fall all three painters were in Saragossa. Goya probably brought Josefa along to share his pleasure at returning home as a success, a full-fledged Academician.

It was not long before difficulties set in. Word spread that Goya was being haughty, proud and intractable in his dealings with Bayeu, who was, after all, the director of the project. Goya, now an Academy Fellow, undoubtedly found the suggestions his brother-in-law made for improving his work degrading and insulting. Their private quarrel quickly became public. Bayeu may have seen Goya's growing skills as a threat to his own position, and he may also have been seeking to pull back under his influence a formerly docile disciple who was suddenly asserting himself in an unwonted fashion. In any case, he told members of the cathedral's Council that he could not, in conscience, take responsibility for the younger artist's work. He put it to them—if they found it acceptable he would say no more, but he could not endorse it. Bayeu's reputation supported his opinion, and the committee viewed Goya's work through his eyes. They demanded corrections on the ceiling and refused to approve Goya's sketches for other unfinished work unless Bayeu sanctioned them first.

Goya was angry, and with Zapater's assistance he drafted a lengthy petition to the Council. Goya begged the committee to submit his work to inspection by a recognized authority, naming several Academicians from Madrid. He even offered to pay for such a judge's trip to Saragossa. But his appeal went unheeded. Goya was ready to quit Saragossa, uncompensated and in disgust, since those of its citizens who cared about such matters sided with Bayeu. But then he received a letter from a Carthusian friar, Félix Salcedo, with whom he had become friends years before when he was painting the frescoes at the monastery of Aula Dei. The friar advised the artist that "there is in man no more noble, Christian and religious act than to humble oneself to another when reason and God's law ask it. . . ." To this general moral advice, Salcedo added some practical counsel: "Today Francisco (Bayeu) is the most outstanding in the Council's esteem and on the eve of being First Painter to the King; you (even though of greater ability) are but beginning now and have not yet won their esteem. . . . You must with complete generosity and Christian charity subject your sketches to Bayeu's judgment. If he wants to avenge himself by discrediting you (which I do not believe), everyone would then know the difference of heart between Bayeu and Goya, and there would be justice."

The friar's mixture of salving flattery, practical advice and appeal to honor struck home. Goya agreed to submit fresh sketches and to fix the dome. By the end of May 1781, he had finished his work. Entitled *Virgin, Queen of Martyrs,* it is generally regarded as superior to the ceilings of his relatives—richer in color and more novel in the arrangement of its principal figures, which are drawn with a powerful realism of which the Bayeus were incapable. Still, there were some petty unpleasantnesses to get through. Goya wished to return to Madrid and so demanded payment the instant he finished. Evidently he was so insistent on the point that the Council snappishly paid him off, stipulating that under no circumstances would he be permitted to continue on the balance of the paintings for the church. They added insult to insult by rewarding all the Bayeus present (both brothers and Goya's wife!) with silver medals, while pointedly ignoring Goya himself. "On remembering Saragossa and painting I burn alive," he later wrote.

But ambition burned still more brightly. Goya was hardly back in Madrid before he was laying plans for a triumph that would more than compensate for the troubles he had encountered in Saragossa. The King had announced a competition to choose seven artists to decorate the Church of San Francisco el Grande, and Goya resolved not only to be one of the winners but also to have his work judged the best of the best when it was viewed among the other's works at the unveiling. Such a victory would, he felt, insure his appointment as Painter to the King. He did no less than three sketches before finally submitting one for approval. In September his pains were rewarded—he received one of the commissions for the church.

His hoped for public triumph was to be postponed some three years because of delays in construction of the church building, and then it was not to be as unclouded a victory as he might have hoped. But he put the interval to good use—to extremely good use—and in January 1783 his efforts were rewarded by the commission of his dreams. He was to paint a portrait of the Prime Minister, the Count of Floridablanca *(page 61).*

Goya could not contain his elation, and he wrote to Zapater: "Although Count Floridablanca has advised me to say nothing, my wife knows, and I also want you alone to know, that I am to paint his portrait, which can be of great advantage to me." A short while later he again wrote his friend: "On this day I have put in the head of the portrait . . . in his presence and have succeeded in getting a good likeness and he is very content."

Perhaps at first he was, for surely this was Floridablanca as he must have liked to see himself, a man of confident power in full regalia. A medal decorates the breast of his gorgeous red satin suit, which is heavily trimmed in the same gold that also decorates his silken waistcoat. The great man's secretary hovers anxiously at his shoulder, awaiting his command, while Goya himself is seen at the left, obsequiously offering a painting for the Prime Minister's inspection. On the wall behind the count, almost concealed by shadows, is a portrait of his sovereign. None of this attracts Floridablanca's attention. He stares fixedly ahead, as if focused on his nation's destiny—or perhaps his own—and he is not to be distracted by trivia. As a token of his devotion to the task, and in his enthusiasm to please this influential client, Goya loaded the picture with the paraphernalia of Floridablanca's wide-ranging interests. Strewn about the floor and the covered table are books, documents and maps—among them, a plan for the canal system of the province of Aragon, which Floridablanca had sponsored. A heavy gilt clock, a rich, Oriental carpet and a thick drape complete the decor. To complicate things further, Goya employed a difficult lighting scheme, which mysteriously illuminates only the count and has no visible source. Goya had not mastered all the intricacies he felt compelled to include.

The picture is very grand, but rather mannered and lacking in the passionate objectivity and compulsion for truth-telling that mark the great stream of portraits that was to begin only a short while later. In this, his first genuinely important commission, Goya is all too obviously attempting to show off his technical skills, his willingness to follow fashion and, above all, his desire to flatter a great man. Goya undoubtedly felt a certain kinship with Floridablanca. He, too, was of humble origins and had struggled up through the Spanish bureaucracy only at the cost of making the most powerful enemies among the aristocracy and the military, who resented both his birth and his liberalism. (A measure of the latter was his secret support, as Minister of Finance, of the American revolution, to which he gave money and arms. In this it is possible that Floridablanca and Spain were more interested in the inconvenience the insurrection caused the traditional English enemy than in the ideals of the cause.) Distrusting his adversaries, he avoided all contact with them and extended this frigid style to almost everyone else as well. "One spends entire weeks vainly seeking an opportunity to speak with him," the Russian ambassador noted, "and when at last one thinks one has seized the favorable moment, he suddenly interrupts the conversation under some trifling pretext, and once more advises you to address him in writing." It is this sense of isolation, of haughty (or was it fearful?) withdrawal from ordinary human contact that Goya's portrait most successfully captures.

Unfortunately, however, Goya's ardent pursuit of the minister, in which he may have been aided by Floridablanca's wife, ended in disappointment. He got his sittings, of course, and mild praise as the work progressed, but when he presented the finished picture, Floridablanca was no more than coldly correct in his response. Busy man that he was, he dismissed the painter briefly: "Goya," he said, "we will clear this up later." It is not recorded that they did, and, in fact, Goya was unable to collect his fee. "Everyone is astonished that nothing should have come from the Minister of State," Goya wrote Zapater. "If nothing comes from that direction, there is nothing more to hope for; and the disappointment is so much the greater when one has had such great hopes."

Luckily, however, Goya had put to good use those warmer, more relaxed moments during the sittings. It was apparently in the course of them that Goya won from the Prime Minister an introduction to the King's youngest brother, the Infante, Don Luis de Bourbon.

Don Luis was, in a minor way, a tragic figure. Made a cardinal before he was 10 years old, he had given up both the cardinal's hat and the Archbishopric of Toledo, thus renouncing his churchly duties and forfeiting the enormous ecclesiastical revenues that went along with them— a not inconsiderable sum, which included income from all of Mexico. Being an "ordinary sensual man," in his own words, he could not bear the celibate life anymore than he could bring himself to submit to the intrigues necessary to circumvent his vow of chastity. When he married, at 35, it was for love and beauty. Forbidden by his brother to marry the daughter of a sovereign or a grandee of Spain—probably to put Don Luis' heirs outside the line of royal succession—the Infante chose the beautiful Doña Maria Teresa de Vallabriga, who belonged to a noble family of Aragon. But, having married morganatically, Don Luis was forced to live in what amounted to an unspoken exile from his brother's court in Madrid. Indeed, after his death in 1785, Maria Teresa was forbidden to live in Madrid or in any other provincial capital and could, of course, reside at none of the royal residences. To make sure that everyone knew his place, the King persisted in calling Don Luis' daughter "cousin," rather than niece. (It is she whom we shall encounter later under the most disheartening of circumstances, and who was to be the subject of one of Goya's greatest portraits.)

In August and September of 1783 Goya visited Don Luis at his re treat in Arenas de San Pedro, southwest of Madrid. A wise egoist often mistaken for a philosopher, Don Luis spent his time puttering about Arenas, interesting himself in botany and the arts and indulging his family's passion for hunting. Goya found him as congenial as Floridablanca had been chilly. "I have gone hunting twice with His Highness," Goya reported, "and the last afternoon he told me, on shooting a rabbit, 'this dauber is even more mad about hunting than I.' " While there, working rapidly, Goya produced a portrait of the Infante and his family (pages 62-63) as well as individual portraits of Don Luis, his wife and two of their young children. (The boy, who was named after his father, eventually accepted the ecclesiastical positions that the Infante had relinquished.)

During his stay at Arenas de San Pedro, Goya probably managed to put in a good word for his priestly brother, for Camillo later obtained from the Infante a post as chaplain at nearby Chinchón. As a parting gift, the family bestowed upon Goya a gown, "all in silver and gold," for his wife. Running to the servant's quarters to obtain an estimate of its worth, Goya was astonished to discover that it was valued at 30,000 reales— about $7,500 in modern terms. "They regretted my departure so much," the bedazzled artist wrote, "that they could only say farewell on condition that I had to return at least once a year." (Unfortunately for Goya, it was a condition that the Infante's death all too soon precluded.) "If I could tell you in detail the things that have happened here, you would be very pleased," Goya wrote. "I have been here a month continually with these señores and they are some angels. . . ."

The Courtly Patrons

As a young, unknown painter, Goya's ambition for recognition and wealth burned as fiercely as his blazing natural talent. A provincial with a modest education, Goya saw the Royal Palace in Madrid with its glitter, pomp and lucrative commissions as the logical place to earn his reputation. Through his brother-in-law, Francisco Bayeu, he secured an appointment as a designer for the Royal Tapestry Manufactory in Madrid. But his great opportunity came in 1783 when, at 37, he was commissioned to do a portrait of the powerful Count of Floridablanca, the Prime Minister *(right)*. The count seems never to have paid Goya for his work, but through him the painter met the Infante Don Luis, brother of King Charles III. The portraits Goya made of the amiable Infante and his family launched him on a distinguished—and highly profitable—career.

Goya's first portraits were uneven, even timid in their desire to flatter the sitter, but with experience his self-confidence grew. Through the years he mastered not only the necessary techniques—composition, color, the use of light—but, above all, he developed a remarkable ability to reveal in a portrait the essential personality of his subject. By 1800, when he was 54, his art had achieved greatness, a judgment that he amply proved in his masterful, *The Family of Charles IV*. By that time, too, Goya had reached the goal his desire for position had set: he was First Painter to the King.

Goya's first important portrait betrays the artist's wish to please. The count dominates a scene filled with details relating to his interests. His secretary and Goya himself stand in the shadows. Although the picture veils Goya's skill in painting what he sees in people, it admirably depicts the importance of this gentleman.

The Count of Floridablanca, 1783

Goya's first enthusiastic and sympathetic patron among the aristocracy was the Infante Don Luis de Bourbon, younger brother of Charles III. On orders from his brother, the Infante lived, with his family and staff, away from the court in a villa southwest of Madrid. During the summer of 1783 Goya stayed for four weeks at the villa, painting portraits of the family. The visit was apparently pleasant for both host and guest: the artist and the Infante shared a love of hunting, and Goya, perhaps grateful to be among the select, painted the Infante's family with warmth and understanding.

His most compelling work is this group portrait of the entire household. The scene is unusual; the Infante's wife is shown having her hair coifed while the family and staff, including the guest, Goya, look on. The Infante is seated; his eldest daughter watches Goya paint while the baby girl is held by a nurse.

The painting itself shows Goya breaking away from his early desire to flatter as he gropes toward revealing the characters of his subjects. He is charitable with these patrons, but he also transmits the relaxed air of a household in which the easy pace of aristocratic life prevailed.

The Family of the Infante Don Luis de Borbón, 1783

63

The Duke and Duchess of Osuna With Their Children, 1789

The Marchioness of Pontejos, c.1786

Foremost among Goya's many society patrons were the Osunas, gracious and wealthy benefactors of actors, bullfighters and artists. Goya completed many pictures for the Osunas, among them an affectionate family portrait *(left)*. To focus attention on his sitters, he placed them against a plain backdrop. A more formal, but no less skilled portrait *(above)* shows the Marchioness of Pontejos, bride of the brother of Count Floridablanca, in a rustic setting. Painted earlier, the picture is rather stilted, and the lady's pose, expensive French silk gown and powdered hair provide a sharp contrast to the *maja* style affected by some of Goya's other subjects.

The Duchess of Alba, 1795

When Goya was 46, his flourishing career was halted violently by a disease that nearly killed him and robbed him of his hearing. After a lengthy recuperation he resumed painting and found a new and an ardent patroness, the beautiful Duchess of Alba, the subject of two of his finest portraits. Whether Goya and the Duchess ever had a full-fledged love affair may never be known—but he was clearly infatuated both by her beauty and by the exciting, flighty personality of this woman.

Goya's first portrait of the Duchess of Alba *(above, left)*

The Duchess of Alba, 1797

captures her vivacity in lively colors. The second portrait was painted two years later *(above, right)* after Goya and the Duchess had spent some pleasant months on her estate in southern Spain. She is dressed in black, the color of mourning—her husband had recently died—but the dress style is also that of a coquettish *maja.* The Duchess wears two rings, one that says, "Alba," and the other, "Goya." She points to an inscription in the sand, "Solo Goya" (Only Goya), one of the few clues that their relationship was more than that of patron and artist.

The Naked Maja, c.1800

Who is this voluptuous woman dressed in a gauzy, form-fitting harem outfit in one picture and naked for the world to see in the other? She is sultry, desirable, seductively immodest as she casts her eyes directly at the viewer, ashamed of nothing. Yet what is her name? Most people would answer, "the Duchess of Alba," for no legend in art has more indelibly impressed itself upon the public imagination than the romantic notion that during his supposed affair with the Duchess, Goya memorialized her in these two pictures. Alas, this is not the case. More convincing speculation is that the model for the paintings may have been a mistress of Manuel Godoy, prime minister and lover of Queen Maria Luisa, for both paintings were listed in the inventory of Godoy's estate. But this is only circumstantial evidence, and it has done little to change the popular belief that the model was the Duchess. Indeed, as recently as 1945 the Alba family, wishing finally to disassociate the Duchess' name from the pictures, agreed to have her body exhumed to compare the measurements of the skeleton with those of the *maja* in the painting. The results proved inconclusive; in fact, the only interesting discovery was that both the Duchess' legs had been broken, probably when her casket was dropped during a French raid on the cemetery at the time of the Napoleonic wars.

In the end, regardless of her true identity, the *maja* has become one of the most admired women in the world. The nude study by Goya is one of the most provocative and magnetic figures ever painted. Furthermore, it is astonishing that the painting was ever done, for nudes were extremely rare in Spanish art; one of the few, and one of the finest nudes in all Western painting, is Velázquez' *Venus*. But Goya's *maja* is no goddess, nor is she a soberly realistic anatomical study—she is a living female, real beyond doubt, yet alluringly romanticized.

Not all of Spanish society appreciated *The Naked Maja*; the artist was called up before the Inquisition when the subject of the painting became known. The results of Goya's trial are not known, but his works were never banned nor was he sent to jail—probably one of his highly placed patrons came to his defense. And Goya, who seemed to court controversy but always avoided its fatal embrace, never revealed who the *maja* really was.

The Clothed Maja, c.1800

María Teresa de Borbón y Vallabriga, Countess of Chinchón, 1783

Countess of Chinchón, 1800

During Goya's lengthy career as a society portraitist, he watched some stories unfold around his patrons that were like fairy tales. One such concerned the eldest daughter of the Infante Don Luis. When she was a little girl, Goya painted her twice: once alone *(left)* and once as a curious child watching him paint his group portrait of her family *(pages 62-63)*. When she was 18, she was married off to the libidinous and despicable Manuel Godoy. The poor girl was all but crushed psychologically by Godoy *(below)* and even in pregnancy she could find little source of pride, as is shown by one of Goya's most poignant portraits *(below, left)*. But the story ends happily; the countess abandoned Godoy after his downfall during the Napoleonic wars, and fled to Cádiz with other aristocrats. There, it is said, she stood on a balcony and sang the popular Spanish song, "Death to Napoleon!"

Don Manuel de Godoy, Duke of Alcudia, Prince of the Peace, 1801

The acceptance of Goya's work by nobles close to the royal circle finally gained for him the title he had sought for years: in 1799 Charles IV named him First Painter to the King. By this time Goya had a great many patrons among the aristocracy and a very comfortable financial position. His illness, however, and his ever-deepening awareness of his art had made him restless. He had already produced his *Caprichos;* even their unsuccessful publication did not lessen his desire to withdraw from society painting, no matter how lucrative it was. He wished to turn to the more imaginative challenges of his private world.

This was the background when the King commissioned Goya to paint a group portrait of the Royal Family. Sketching likenesses of some members of the family individually, and with occasional group poses, Goya worked quickly and finished the painting within a year. The result is a triumph: the costumes of the family glitter with the wealth and ostentation of their rank, yet the faces of the King and Queen betray their shocking lack of character. So drab does this splendidly dressed couple seem that the French novelist Théophile Gautier observed that they looked like "the corner baker and his wife after they have won the lottery."

There was little about the personalities of this spiteful family that escaped Goya's eye and brush. The haughty, arrogant man in blue at the left is the King's eldest son, who was later to become the tyrant Ferdinand VII. Beside him is a girl with her face averted, his bride-to-be who had not yet been officially affianced. Queen Maria Luisa, flanked by her youngest children, is the focal point of the painting, while the King stands to one side, as he did in life, almost in deference to her. Other lesser relatives are grouped behind the King. Perhaps in imitation of Velázquez' invention in the masterpiece *Las Meninas,* and as he had done in previous pictures, Goya shows himself working diligently in the background.

The Family of Charles IV, 1800

Only an artist like Goya, supremely confident of his talent and perhaps wealthy enough to risk losing his job as First Painter to the King, could have dared paint so truthful a portrait of royal personages as is seen in the detail at right from *The Family of Charles IV*. Here it becomes clear just how realistically he had portrayed Queen Maria Luisa. Nothing unflattering is toned down or omitted; her double chin and thick neck are conspicuous; her expression is coarse, almost vulgar; her arms, which Goya knew she admired for their plumpness, are full to the point of grossness. By contrast, her young daughter, Doña Maria Isabel, is angelic; her jewelry, dress and eyes are very much like her mother's, but she radiates a soft pleasantness, a mark not only of her own uncorrupted youth but of Goya's affinity for children.

Goya's true-to-life portrait probably shocked no one; even the Queen on occasion had made light of her ugliness, perhaps expecting to be contradicted. The royal couple expressed neither displeasure nor enthusiasm over the work. And although Goya never painted for the King and Queen again, it was apparently not because they were dissatisfied. In any case, Goya had gained fame at the court, and his interests now turned more to fulfilling his own artistic needs. In 1802 the Duchess of Alba died, symbolically closing the period in Goya's life when he painted for the pleasure of the rich and powerful in Madrid.

Doña Maria Isabel and Queen Maria Luisa. Detail from *The Family of Charles IV*.

74

76

IV

Painter to the King

Goya's portrait of the Duke of
Alba shows him in his
characteristic role of devotee of
the arts; he leans on a beautifully
made harpsichord and holds a
copy of a musical work by Haydn,
the German composer with
whom he was friendly. The
modest Duke was often lost in the
dazzle of his flamboyant wife; he
was even obliged by her and her
family to take her name—Alba—
when they wed.

The Duke of Alba, c.1795

Goya was 37 years old in 1783 and was reaching toward the fulfill-
ment of all his worldly ambitions. The portraits of the Infante Don Luis
and his family completed the process of establishing him as the most
fashionable artist of his time and place. In the next year one important
commission after another flowed to him. Portraits, religious paintings,
mythological allegories tumbled out of his studio as the best people
sought his services. A friendship with Jovellanos, a leading figure of the
Spanish Enlightenment, quickened and deepened, and through him
Goya obtained a commission for four pictures for the University of Sala-
manca. Another important client, the Duke of Hijar, paid him 3,000
reales for a painting to be placed in a parish church in the province of Te-
ruel. There were paintings of *Cupid and Psyche*, of *Hercules and Omphale*,
a portrait of a prominent architect, Don Ventura Rodriguez, and then at
the end of 1784, two supreme events occurred.

The first was the birth of the one child who was to survive Goya—"a
very healthy and sturdy boy," baptized Francisco Xavier Pedro. "The
confinement was not difficult," Goya added when he wrote to Zapater,
"I trust to God this time it will go well." He had reason to worry, for
during this period, when he was striving so hard for success, Goya was
afflicted with an uncommon number of family tragedies that may have
contributed to the darkness that was to shadow his artistic vision. As his
letter suggests, a number of his children had died at birth or soon thereafter. Furthermore, in 1781 his father had died, followed very shortly by
his sister, Rita. But the birth of a thriving son reversed his feelings of de-
spondency, at least temporarily. Throughout the years Goya lavished on
the boy an immoderate affection and was forever concerned, almost obsessively, with providing him a patrimony that would match that
affection. The portrait he painted of Xavier when he was 19 is a mark of
that love and an infinitely more tender evocation than the surviving portrait of his wife, Josefa. Indeed, it is one of the great studies of youth
caught in a moment of transition between adolescence and manhood.
The pose is that of a would-be worldling. Xavier leans nonchalantly, like
a dandy, on a walking stick—a picture of studied ease. But the face is still

that of a boy—the soft line of his chin has not yet hardened into a mature set, his lips are delicate; the eyes essay a certain boldness but betray innocence and unspoken questions. It is, in short, a very loving and very understanding portrait, and it summarizes Goya's feelings for the youth who he must have felt could assure his immortality in a way that no work of art ever could.

Goya's happiness at Xavier's birth was capped, just six days later, by the King's unveiling, at long last, of the seven altar paintings for the Church of San Francisco el Grande. (Coincidentally, the King's son and daughter-in-law had just produced the long-awaited male heir who might assure the succession of *his* line.) Goya's contribution to the church decorations—a picture of St. Bernard preaching—has not been treated kindly by later critics, one of whom suggested that the composition had been borrowed from a French artist and declared that "from the whole boring mass only the self-portrait [which Goya had inserted into the background] stands out . . . the solid and robust head of the artist." Count Floridablanca was present at the unveiling on the great day and was his usual indifferent self. Fortunately, Goya seems to have been unaware of the Prime Minister's lack of enthusiasm and, of course, was ignorant of history's judgment. Instead, he heard all around him the sweet sound of popular approval. Most people, indeed, thought his was the best of the seven paintings—just as he had hoped from the beginning. "I have had good luck with my St. Bernard, according to the judgment of the audience as well as that of the general public," he wrote Zapater. "Without reservation, they are all for me."

Undoubtedly this success brought him still more commissions. It also brought him some immediate frustrations. Goya and two other artists who lacked official titles as Painters to the King had not received advance payments on the church paintings. Unlike their colleagues, who held royal positions and drew salaries for doing this sort of work, Goya and the other two were dependent on the Crown for prompt payment of their fees. For some reason, these were not immediately forthcoming. The artists forwarded a petition to Floridablanca, and the secretary of the Royal Academy of San Fernando added to the petition a plea for quick, favorable action "so that these poor fellows may not be discouraged, and that the recompense may inspire them to other works." They won their case, but the Prime Minister had the last, disdainful word. He scrawled in the margin of their petition, "Although the pictures are not worth much of anything, those of these three are still the least bad."

By this time, however, even Floridablanca's indifference could not hold Goya back. Hoping for an appointment as assistant director of the Academy, he settled for the post of deputy director of its division of painting. It brought "little profit and much honor," he sourly complained to Zapater, noting that he would have to devote considerable time to teaching classes of aspiring artists. Still, the job represented progress and another increase in his reputation. Moreover, new commissions were coming in most satisfactorily. He painted a lovely *Annunciation* for San Antonio del Prado in Madrid at the behest of the Duke of Medinaceli, head of one of the nation's great families. Even more significant was his introduction into the household of the Duke and Duchess of Osuna.

Lady Holland, an Englishwoman whose journal of her stay in Spain is the source of much information about life at the Spanish court in this period, called the Duchess "the most distinguished woman in Madrid, for her talents, worth and taste." Twice a princess, seven or eight times a duchess, the blood of the Borgia mingled in her veins with that of many of the great Spanish families. She was married to her first cousin, who was neither as energetic nor as intelligent as she was. Indeed, it might be said that the elegant Duchess of Osuna—angular, stiffly tense in manner —lacked only beauty and, perhaps, a certain modesty about her many attainments. A famous horsewoman, she would spend days alone riding over her estates, accepting for company anyone of any rank whom she chanced upon, with "no fear of storms, or of marauders." She was also one of the most devoted followers of the bullfights and enjoyed mingling not only with matadors, but also with poets, writers, actors, artists and other types not ordinarily granted intimate entrée to company as exalted as hers. Moreover—and this was truly unheard of among women of her class—she had serious ambitions as an intellectual. She was fully capable of managing her own estates, was President of the Woman's Section of the Economic Society of Madrid, and drew tremendously influential audiences to her frequent lectures on the most formidable aspects of this new, and newly fashionable, science. She also fancied herself something of an actress and, despite the awkwardness of her bearing, frequently mounted the small stage at her magnificent country home, the Alameda. There she would perform in plays created for her by the well-known poet Don Tomás de Yriarte, whom she kept on her staff specifically to provide entertainments for the assemblage of aristocrats and untitled men of talent—or at least notoriety—whom she delighted in mixing on her guest lists.

It was for the Alameda that Goya created some of his most charming paintings—seven bright, anecdotal scenes of popular life that must have seemed like windows on the outside world in the country house. Of the estate itself, Lady Holland noted, "Alameda very pretty, fitted up with great elegance by the Duchess, but created at an immense expense. Gardens contrived for coolness, innumerable grottoes, temples, *chaumières* [thatched cottages], hermitages, excavations, canal, ports, pleasure boats, islands, mounts, etc. etc." Goya was obviously living a princely life at the Osunas. And his pleasures must have been increased by his hostess, whom Lady Holland further described as "very agreeable; great natural talents, wit, eloquence and vivacity."

She created scandal, of course. And she had her rivals, among them the youthful and beautiful Duchess of Alba. Nor was she above responding with singular harshness to attacks upon her style of life. The author of a satirical almanac who alluded to some of her foibles—well-known through gossip—was banished from court for his indiscretion. A writer of satirical songs who hinted at her rivalry with the Duchess of Alba got a year in jail for his pains. But she was not always capricious. Once Goya had painted the Duchess and her husband, she never wavered in her loyalty to him, not even after his celebrated friendship with the Duchess of

Goya painted his only surviving child, Xavier, in 1803 when the handsome youth was 19. Generously, Goya arranged for his son to receive a royal pension, got him a government job and, when Xavier married in 1805, moved to a larger house so that he could offer a home to the young couple. But Xavier was a lazy nonentity: he quit his post a year after being appointed, moved out of his parents' home six months after his marriage and lived the rest of his 69 years in idleness, enjoying his pension, an annuity the Duchess of Alba left him, and the property and large sums of money his father deeded and willed to him.

Alba began. Moreover, she was a generous patroness. Goya received 1,000 reales for each preparatory sketch he made for a portrait of the Osuna family and 12,000 reales for the finished work—the equivalent of an entire year's income for him at that time. The Osunas, indeed, were the greatest private purchasers of his work; only the Royal Family exceeded them in patronizing Goya.

And yet it cannot be said that Goya's initial sketches of the Duke and his lady are obsequious in their flattery. In the family portrait *(page 64)* with their children grouped around them, there is a certain sentimentality. The face of the Duchess does not reveal quite the strength of will that memorialists ascribe to her. Still, Goya does not invest the woman with a physical grace she did not possess; the Duke appears no stronger than he actually was, and neither can he be regarded as particularly handsome. If there is idealization in the picture it is in the lovely, pensive faces of the children and in the loving care with which Goya painted everyone's dress —a device that he, like many portraitists, used when he wanted to distract his patrons from whatever psychological penetration he accomplished with his brush.

The other quality one notes in this picture, as in so many others of this period, is the radical simplification of background, which was new to Goya and was to become one of the most characteristic qualities of his portraiture. A plain backdrop, the colors a light, shimmering gray, blue or green—these were the materials with which he filled out his canvases. Rarely again would he toy with the trivial complexities of detail that marred his portrait of Floridablanca; nothing would be allowed to distract the viewer from contemplation of his subject.

The 18th Century was, of course, a great age of portraiture. Goya was probably beginning to study the work of his renowned English contemporaries, Joshua Reynolds, George Romney and Thomas Gainsborough, and like them Goya was intent on capturing something more than merely an accurate likeness when he set out to paint an individual from life. No less than a landscape artist, he was attempting to plumb the secrets of nature as it was revealed in the expressions of his sitters. His way to the truth was not that of Reynolds, who advised the artist that "instead of endeavoring to amuse mankind with the minute neatness of his imitations, he must endeavor to improve them by the grandeur of his ideas." Nature in her normally imperfect state would thus be idealized by reference to her rarer, more perfect moments. Goya's way, however, was that of William Hogarth, whose engravings he may also have known. Like Hogarth, he tried to paint people as he saw them, with their foibles and follies exposed under a ruthlessly honest gaze. Beyond the fine exterior and momentary grandeur they donned with their posing costume, Goya perceived the isolation of the individual.

It was hard work. And it demanded a certain daring on Goya's part. His subjects, after all, were paying for likenesses, not for truth. Yet Goya prospered mightily from it; no instance is recorded of a patron having rejected his portrait because it did not flatter. Perhaps the Spaniards had a greater tolerance for frankness in these matters than did their neighbors in the north of Europe, for it is hard to imagine Reynolds' elegant sitters accepting paintings such as those marked by Goya's forthrightness.

In 1786, somewhat reconciled with his brother-in-law, Goya painted a magnificent portrait of Bayeu, all pearly grays and very austere. The older man is still seen as the stern taskmaster of Goya's youth, though now with just a hint of condescension and, perhaps, contempt. Other portraits followed: there was Floridablanca's sister-in-law, the Marchioness de Pontejos *(page 65)*, a flower drooping from her hand, a pug dog glowering at her feet, a wonderful stillness about the subject herself. Finally, there was the standing portrait of King Charles III himself *(page 43)* in hunting garb—a small, mahogany man, long-nosed, smiling engagingly at some secret of his own. It is as affectionate a portrait of royalty as the world has ever seen.

Goya had reason to feel affection, for in this year he was finally able

Self-portrait, c. 1786

to write: "Martín, I am now Painter to the King, with 15,000 reales!" Goya's name was once again linked with Ramón Bayeu who received a similar post at the same time. In effect, the appointment merely placed him on salary to do what he had been doing on commission—the tapestry cartoons. But it did carry with it the obligation to do "what may be required in the palace in fresco and oils," and increased the range of his royal work.

It also increased the pace of his work. "I am so up to my ears at this moment," Goya wrote in 1786, "that I do not know which way to turn and especially how to fulfill all the engagements I have accepted." Around this time he painted a self-portrait *(page 81)* that reveals one of the methods by which he was attempting to crowd more hours into his working day. He shows himself at his easel, in a tight-fitting costume that reveals his strong, chunky legs and his solid torso. On his head he wears a round, comical hat, on the brim of which are placed a number of small candles to illuminate his canvas as he works on into the night. A self-satisfied, faintly wicked expression plays about his features, as if he enjoyed exposing his clever solution to the problem of working by artificial light and the eccentricity of his professional habits.

A fast pace suited Goya's temperament. He was capable of the most delicate brushwork, particularly when working with flesh tones and textures. (On close examination the faces of some of his portrait subjects seem blurred and out of focus, and neither the definitive line of a wrinkle nor the trace of the artist's brush can be discerned: it is as if Goya had found a way of rendering the imperceptible movement of breathing.) But his most characteristic stroke was short, rapid, fairly heavy and rather nervous. Indeed, one of Goya's great contributions to the technique of painting lay in breaking up the long, smooth curve—both in a painted and a drawn line—the arabesque that was the hallmark of Baroque and Rococo styles. And when he approached a canvas, Goya almost always painted directly—often for 10 hours at a stretch—without making careful preliminary studies. It is true that he sometimes produced quick sketches of various details of a painting beforehand, but only a half-dozen or so full compositional studies are known. In addition, Goya seldom overpainted. Explaining why he did not indulge in extensive retouching, he said that "it is not easy to retain the imagination's immediate, transitory intention and the harmony of the first execution." In his preference for transferring ideas and insights to canvas as quickly and purely as possible, he was a precursor of the rebellious Romantic painters of the 19th Century, many of whom—Delacroix in particular—acknowledged his influence. But of most immediate importance to him was the fact that with this method of work he was able to accept and execute huge numbers of commissions. It is fair to say that much of his prosperity was based on his facility.

Now in his late thirties, the rewards were commensurate with his efforts. He moved out of the crowded central district of Madrid and bought a little house with a garden and a broad vista across the Manzanares River, which flows through Madrid and on whose banks the home was situated. Immediately after receiving his appointment as Painter to the King, he bought a two-wheeled cabriolet. It was a sporty affair, too light for safety, but it suited Goya's dashing and individualistic image of himself. There were only three such vehicles in all Madrid. Unfortunately, Goya overturned it the first time he took it out, injuring his right leg in the accident. Although he limped for some months, he continued to drive the cabriolet for a year or so. Afterwards, he purchased a more conservative four-wheeled carriage, designed to be drawn by two mules and worth over 7,500 reales (about $2,000).

Goya was pleased with his economic and social progress, boasting even as he complained of the new impositions that accompanied his success. "I can't do more than I am doing; my situation is very different from what people imagine," he wrote to Zapater—possibly in an attempt to forestall a trip to Madrid which Goya's brother and sister wished him to sponsor. No matter. He had already boasted that "I have arranged a very agreeable life for myself; I no longer wait around in anterooms; the man who wants something of mine comes to me to seek it, which makes me more wanted; if it is not a person in very high position, or someone recommended by a friend, I do not work for anyone."

Of course, his friends had plenty of friends, and his name was now extremely well regarded by those in high positions. Caught in a flood of work, he often painted superficially. For example, the portraits that he executed of the directors of the Bank of San Carlos were competent, but hardly inspired, though the gentlemen were among the most interesting figures of the Spanish Enlightenment. And, working unevenly and with little originality, he did a set of altar paintings at the behest of the King for the Church of Santa Ana at Valladolid. He approached the job in a spirit best described as dutiful, confessing that, "though I've not yet done a thing on it, it must be done, since the King has ordered it."

Sometimes, in his haste, he did poorly with subjects that should have provided him with the richest sort of material. His patroness, the Duchess of Osuna, was proud of being in direct line of descent from an authentic saint—Francisco Borgia, the fourth Duke of Gandia and third General of the Jesuit order. Her family had built a chapel in his honor in Valencia, and she commissioned Goya to decorate it with scenes from the saint's life.

The legend of Borgia's spiritual conversion was the sort of thing that particularly appealed to the Spanish religious temper. Charged by the Emperor Charles V with transporting a coffin containing the body of the Empress Isabella, one of the most beautiful women of her day, the Duke met with an accident on the road. The coffin broke open, and the corpse spilled out in a state of horrible decomposition. The sight was a revelation to the Duke of the transitory nature of earthly vanity and strivings. Putting aside all that he had valued, leaving family, estates and ease, the Duke set out to find the true path to God.

The terrible paradox of death in the midst of luxurious life, the black irony of the manner in which this truth was revealed to the Duke, these were subjects to which Spanish artists often turned and to which Goya himself would be particularly attracted in later years. Now, however, he contented himself with a bland, even sentimental, evocation of Borgia taking leave of his family before taking his vows. He also did a rather wooden scene, showing the saint exorcising demons from an afflicted sinner. The picture *(page 96)* is interesting chiefly because it is the first time Goya is known to have populated one of his works with those shades of the underworld—half man, half animal—which are so often subjects in his later etchings and in the "Black Paintings." Here they are modest, rather conventional symbols of evil, lacking that urgent, forceful animation of their later incarnations, where they dominate the work as they had come to dominate Goya's mind.

But if Goya was at times guilty of superficial work in this period, if he occasionally missed the opportunities that often lay hidden in some of his commissions, he was also capable—on a similarly erratic basis—of very profound painting. Two excellent examples of his finest work date from these years of first prominence. One is a small thing, about 17 by 37 inches, called *The Festival of San Isidro (pages 18-19),* a preparatory study in oils for a larger tapestry cartoon that he never executed. His sub-

In 1798 Goya painted for the Duke and Duchess of Osuna six canvases on the then popular subject of witchcraft. The *Witches' Sabbath (right)* shows the climax of one of these grisly scenes of necromancy. Satan, in the form of a giant he-goat, his curved horns wreathed with oak leaves, presides over the monstrous rite of child sacrifice, his left forehoof awesomely touching the next victim. Demented hags and pitiful babies— both dead and alive—ring the goat-devil under a pale crescent moon, as huge bats hover overhead. Goya returned to the subject years later, and in a darker mood, in his "Black Paintings."

ject was one of the most popular of Madrid's many religious festivals, and Goya captured its spirit wonderfully. A golden impression of the city itself shimmers like a dream in the distance beyond the Manzanares. Along the river's banks hundreds of people are gathered. Parasols are up; the lace of the ladies' dresses and the peacock colors of masculine finery delight the eye; the revelers' poses bespeak an easy delight in the spring-time sunshine and the end of winter's fevers. It is a picture of marvelous innocence and openness, treated by the artist with a richness and an emphasis quite new to him. Here, in the words of André Malraux, "He is no longer painting a cartoon but a picture."

He seemed to know this himself, for the execution of the tapestry design saw him pressed for time, working with "much persistence and uneasiness," and writing to Zapater that it was a "very difficult thing with so much to be done . . . with all the tumult customary to it in this court. . . . I neither sleep, nor am calm, until finishing it. . . . " It is his first masterpiece.

One more followed close upon it. It is one of his most often reproduced portraits. Commissioned by one of Goya's most enthusiastic patrons during this period, the Count of Altamira, it shows the aristocrat's young son Don Manuel Osorio de Zúñiga *(page 24)*, a small child dressed in a bright red suit with a broad sash and a lace collar. At first glance the boy seems rather stiff. But there is something very right about this attitude, for what child would not be awkward in the unfamiliar situation of posing for an artist while dressed in his best? In the portrait Goya has unforgettably captured the gravity of childhood, and he has suggested, as well, the inevitable ending of its innocence. The boy holds a bird by a string, and three cats, their eyes glittering avidly, stare fixedly at the creature, ready to pounce—symbols of the terrors of the world which will all too soon spring from the shadows and introduce the child to the anxieties and dreads of adulthood.

It may be assumed that Goya, preoccupied by success, was unaware of the hints of impending darkness that were beginning to creep into a few —a very few as yet—of his paintings. Nor was he aware of the fact that the death of Charles III at the end of 1788 marked the end of an all-too-brief period of fresh air and sunshine in the political life of Spain. Undoubtedly he regretted the loss of this good, wise and gentle man— almost everyone did. But once the period of mourning was over, Goya and the rest of the court painters plunged into a round of hectic activity. Portraits of the new king, Charles IV, and his queen, Maria Luisa, were much in demand. The studios of the leading painters virtually became factories, turning out innumerable pictures of the royal couple to decorate the homes of their more prosperous subjects. The Duchess of Osuna, indeed, bade Goya create two giant portraits of the new sovereigns to hang outside her Madrid palace on September 21, 1789, the night the monarch and his wife made their official entry into the capital.

For this night other noble families ordered elaborate triumphal arches to be erected in front of their homes, in their gardens and in public squares. The city of Madrid itself lit no less than 120,000 candles, torches and crystal lanterns, turning the coronation night into glorious day.

In great homes, the celebratory balls went on past sunrise, while commoners, not to be outdone, danced equally long in the city's squares, to music provided at royal command by the best available musicians.

Many would have cause to regret this night of gaiety. The King was a dull and loutish fellow who delighted in bellowing his courtiers into submission, and whose favorite recreation was wrestling with stable hands. Despite his great physical strength, Charles IV was dominated by his conniving, sexually insatiable wife, a woman who would ultimately raise one of her lovers, an officer of the guard named Manuel Godoy, to the status of Prime Minister. Maria Luisa and Godoy, together with the fatuous Crown Prince (ultimately Ferdinand VII), would destroy the Spanish Enlightenment, allow their country to be overrun by foreign troops and, in the process, see it reduced to a state of backwardness and hopelessness at least as dismal as it had suffered at the end of the Habsburg dynasty. In calmer times, Spain might have survived a reign as lunatic as that of Charles and Maria Luisa. But when they became masters of the Royal Palace, the Bastille in Paris had already fallen: Europe's great age of revolution had begun, and this new and mighty historical force would not long tolerate their incompetence.

However nervous Spain was about the events taking place across the Pyrenees, it was not at first directly affected by the French Revolution. The shrewd Floridablanca retained his portfolio as Prime Minister until 1791 (Charles III had, on his deathbed, advised his son never to part with him), and the other men of the Enlightenment also retained their ministries. The people, indeed, liked the bluff, hearty ways of the new King, and Goya had good reason to share their enthusiasm. Even before his coronation, Charles IV rewarded the artist with the post he had so long desired; in April 1789 it was announced that the King "has deigned to name Don Francisco Goya Painter to the Chamber with all the rights which this post enjoys today." The post carried with it an increase in salary over the 15,000 reales he was already receiving and a more direct and personal relationship with the King in regard to new painting assignments. In addition, of course, it was a high honor, shared by only a few other painters in all of Spain.

Only two years before, Goya had written Zapater that "I have become old, with so many wrinkles in my face that you would no longer recognize me if it were not for my flat nose and my sunken eyes. . . . I feel my 41 years very much." But with his new official position, with the commissions continuing to roll in, he did not act like an old man. On the contrary, he had never been more active. A year after his appointment he confirmed the King's judgment by painting a splendid portrait of the sovereign, his first of many. The King engaged him in intimate conversations as the sittings proceeded, inquiring about his beginnings in Saragossa, his private life, even his opinion of the current political situation in Aragon. And when he saw the finished portrait, the King signified his approval, and Goya reported that "with his hands on my shoulders, we half-embraced." And Goya knew that he had won the most important patron available.

There were plenty of others. And a new fame as well. In the summer

During a furious burst of activity between 1797 and 1801, Goya painted a gallery full of portraits of his acquaintances and friends, including this one of his classmate and long-time confidant Martín Zapater, a Saragossan lawyer of private means. Though Goya once wrote Zapater, "Chico, I know that we understand each other in everything," the differences between the court painter and the sedate provincial bourgeois slowly eroded their friendship. All of Goya's letters, the last dated 1801, were kept by Zapater; his nephew published 55 of them in 1868.

of 1790 doctors advised Josefa Goya to escape Madrid for a while, and Goya accompanied her to Valencia, intending to do some hunting. The painters of the area, responding to the presence of a celebrity in their midst, organized a gay picnic in his honor, and it is believed that in this period he did a few nude sketches, though there is endless debate as to who his model was. A little later he visited Saragossa, where he found the opportunity, at long last, to paint his friend, "the good Martín." He dedicated the portrait on the canvas itself, "To my friend Zapater," but could not resist making sure his provincial friend understood the cost of a celebrity's favor: "I have done this portrait for you with a great deal of labor," he said.

More royal portraits followed, along with a fine portrait of the Archbishop of Valencia, the Countess del Carpio and finally the actress, María del Rosario Fernández, "la Tirana" as she was called because her husband specialized in playing tyrants on the stage. Goya captured her in a moment of radiant triumph in a three-quarter length portrait—she had just emerged the victor in a competition with a rival for the theatergoing public's favor—and the picture is especially interesting because a few years later he painted her again, when illness and shifts in public taste had considerably reduced her status. The two portraits form an excellent commentary on Goya's perception of the inner life of his subjects and on the rigors and perils of a public career.

Goya himself was by no means immune to these forces. As early as 1791, intoxicated by the favor he had found at court and bored by the vast number of tapestry cartoons he had already turned out, he began to neglect his commitment to the Tapestry Manufactory. The director of that institution prepared a report criticizing Goya and Ramón Bayeu for failing to deliver designs, and noting that if they did not mend their ways a good many workmen would be unavoidably laid off. Goya replied by pointing out that none of the other Painters to the King's Chamber had to supply cartoons, that he was busy with other royal commissions and thus more than earning his salary. He managed to anger everyone, including the Minister of Finance, with his new intransigence. One last time, Francisco Bayeu had to intervene, soothing feelings and keeping his brother-in-law from disgrace. Goya was grateful, writing that he had "asked God with the greatest fervor to rid me of the spirit that exceeds me on these occasions, so as not to incur anything that resembles arrogance."

God was all too soon to oblige him. Goya completed the last of his cartoons, *The Dummy (page 28)*, in which a group of girls are tossing a life-sized doll in a blanket, and several others—all large and brilliant—which were destined for the King's study at his country palace-monastery, El Escorial. After completing the paintings, Goya decided to take a vacation in Cádiz, visiting his friend Sebastián Martínez, an art collector and government official. A French diplomat of the time described this blue and white city by the sea as "incontestably the most opulent . . . and one of the most beautiful, in Spain." Goya was to be envied his journey there. But not the chastisement that, in His mysterious way, God chose to administer to Goya's pride while he rested at the shore.

A Lively Piety

In 1798, at the peak of his career, Goya received a royal commission to decorate the church of San Antonio de la Florida, newly built at the King's order in the park land between Madrid's walls and the Manzanares River. It was intended to serve customs officials, the city gatekeepers and riverbank washerwomen. For his paintings, which were to be done in fresco, Goya was asked to illustrate a popular legend about the little church's patron saint, the 13th Century Franciscan friar, Anthony of Padua. The legend tells how a murder victim was miraculously restored to life by St. Anthony so that he could swear to the innocence of Anthony's father, the man who had been falsely accused of the killing.

Perhaps because it was not a regular parish church, perhaps because of its isolated site and humble worshipers, Goya was free to invent his own treatment of the theme and felt no need to follow the orthodox formula for church decoration. Instead of filling the dome with the usual heavenly scene of cloud-borne angels and showing St. Anthony's miracle on the walls below the cupola, as convention decreed, Goya turned the formula upside down. He filled the panels and arches below the cupola with cherubs and angels gazing up at the dome where the saint, surrounded by a bustling crowd of very human witnesses, calls the corpse to momentary life. Sure of his technique and confident of his design, Goya completed his dazzling frescoes in less than five months.

In place of the traditional seraphic choirboys, Goya painted a delicate flight of down-to-earth feminine angels dressed in the rich silks and gauzy muslins Spanish girls wore at the end of the 18th Century. Their bright eyes and fair complexions were sharply criticized by prudish critics—one of whom sneered that the women looked like harlots. But the sense of genuine awe and reverence that he communicates in these pretty young people—and in all the figures of the dome—is the more profound for its being human.

Fresco detail, San Antonio de la Florida, 1798

Interior of San Antonio, facing Goya's tomb and the altar

Around the rim of San Antonio's dome, Goya painted a railing that contains and defines the circular sweep of the crowd watching the saint perform the miracle. He set off this colorful, earthy throng against a background of dull grays, greens and blues, bleaching to pure white at the summit of the cupola, as seen in the photograph at left, taken from directly below it. Goya centered the young saint above the altar, drawing the eye to the miracle scene as one enters the church *(above)*. Save for a group of angels adoring the Trinity in the half-dome over the altar, every decorative element is focused up toward the cupola. Above the exquisite angels, Goya painted his crowd reacting to the miracle with such varied emotions that each individual seems familiar. Today the little church is Goya's memorial; a monument over his tomb lies between the steps leading to the altar.

91

Goya achieved the dramatic effect of his fresco by characterizing the reactions of the participants so vividly that they not only tell the legend of St. Anthony, but also reveal something of the spectators' personalities. Dominating the central scene *(above)*, the sober young saint seems to beckon speech from the livid corpse;

Anthony's father, the old man standing above the murder victim, shows the tearful gratitude of a man vindicated of false accusation. In each of the other five figures near St. Anthony, Goya expressed reactions of wonder, from humble piety in the man holding the corpse and a woman's sentimental ecstasy to doubt, anguish and

skepticism in three men in the background. Behind the saint, Goya painted two street urchins climbing the railing to see better and a superstitious soul who is moved to make a sign against sorcery. The real murderer, in black hat and buff jerkin, reveals his guilty panic by trying to escape through the crowd. The group on the following pages watches the miracle scene from the opposite side of the dome. Exalted at the sight, a young man has leapt on a bench—his dazzled face toward heaven. To the right, Goya contrasts a gaudily dressed woman whose face betrays rapt curiosity and a girl in white whose gentle, pensive features are a masterly evocation of tenderness.

93

96

V

The Passionate Duchess

A dying man, haunted by demonic animals who peer from the dark background, is entreated to repent by St. Francis of Borgia. Not a masterpiece, the picture is significant in Goya's development, for it foreshadows his use of grotesque creatures to suggest the dark side of human nature. Such inventions would become a staple part of his art about four years later with his series of etchings, the *Caprichos*.

St. Francis of Borgia Exorcising a Demonized Dying Man, 1788

It was probably in the fall of 1792 in Cádiz that Goya finished his fine portrait of Sebastián Martínez, the friend with whom he was staying, and set forth on the journey homeward to Madrid. But in Seville he was stricken with dizziness and partial paralysis. Recovering temporarily from this first onslaught of his mysterious affliction, he returned to Martínez' home, there to rest for several months before he again felt able to travel.

His friends nervously speculated on the nature of his illness and on his ability to resume his career. Zapater wrote to Bayeu that "Goya's lack of self-concern has brought this on, but still he must be regarded with the compassion that his misfortune demands." And he gloomily confided to Martínez: "As the illness is of the most fearsome nature, it makes me melancholy thinking of his recuperation." No one, probably not even Goya, knew exactly what he suffered from. Modern medical men who have studied records of Goya's symptoms conclude that the artist either was afflicted with neurolabyrinthitis, an inflammation of the nerves of the inner ear, or was suffering from a Vogt-Koyanagi syndrome, evidence of a severe eye infection. Whether or not there was any connection between this illness and his earlier sickness is not known. In any case, the concern of Goya's friends over his professional future was well justified. He languished for about a year, and for a good part of this time he was in a state of almost complete paralysis coupled with total deafness. In February 1794 Jovellanos noted in his journal that he had written to Goya "who answered that as a result of his apoplexy he remained unable even to write." A couple of months later Goya wrote Zapater, "I am the same in regard to my health, at times suffering dreadful pain with a disposition that even I can't put up with, and at other times milder, as now when I have taken the pen to write to you, and already I tire. . . ." As critic André Malraux later observed of this period, "One of the charming artists of the 18th Century was expiring."

And so he was. But from the ruin of that charm a new artist was to arise. By the time he was writing gloomily to Jovellanos and Zapater, the paralysis, at least, had passed, and the blindness Goya feared more than anything had not come. He was, however, left with complete and incurable deafness; the only sounds that penetrated his consciousness for the rest of his life were frightful, unearthly buzzings capable of driving him close to madness. Still, both inward and outward demands compelled him to go on working, and by July 1793 he felt strong enough to appear at a meeting of the Royal Academy of San Fernando in Madrid. Around that time he also returned to his easel. By January 1794 he was writing to Bernardo Yriarte, the brother of Tomás, that "to occupy the imagination vexed by the consideration of my illnesses, and to compensate in part for the great wastes of time they have caused me, I have dedicated myself to painting a group of cabinet pictures in which I have succeeded in making observations that ordinarily find no place in commissioned works, in which caprice and invention are not given much freedom."

There is doubt as to just which pictures were included in this series. It is known only that with his letter to Yriarte Goya sent 11 small paintings of "various popular diversions," which were at once exhibited at the Academy. The members were much pleased on seeing them, "celebrating their merit and that of Goya." The artist had indicated that Yriarte might keep them as long as he liked, and so after the exhibition the paintings were returned to Yriarte's home. The subsequent history of the series is obscure, but it seems likely that four of the five small masterpieces that today hang in the Royal Academy of Fine Arts in Madrid—*The Procession of Flagellants, An Inquisition Scene, The Burial of the Sardine, The Village Bullfight (page 161)*—were among the originals. While it may seem inappropriate to classify these as "popular diversions," to do so requires only a little stretch of an imagination as fevered as Goya's was at that time. They are certainly composed with "caprice and invention," and they represent a change in style comparable to the change in emotional climate that his illness had wrought in Goya.

On the other hand, some scholars feel that his line in these works is too heavy, the brushstrokes too short for them to have been done at this early time. They add also that a sickly and anxious Goya would have been unlikely to risk the wrath of the Inquisition by painting it at work, that the tradition of penitents parading through the streets beating themselves in an excess of religious fervor was in disfavor with the government at the time and therefore also an unlikely subject for Goya to undertake. But these pictures better suit Goya's description of his work in progress than any others known. Moreover, there is documentary evidence that the fifth picture presently in the Academy, *The Madhouse (page 21)*, was painted at this time. It would have qualified as a "popular diversion" since it was then an almost universal custom in Europe to visit asylums to find amusement in the peculiar behavior of the inmates. But Goya did not exhibit this work at the Academy; instead he sent it to Yriarte a little later, describing it as "a corral of madmen and two who are fighting, nude, with their keeper beating them and others with sacks (a subject which I witnessed in Saragossa)."

In some ways *The Madhouse* is the most logically motivated of all these paintings. In his illness Goya had been at least for moments—and perhaps for hours and even days—mad. He had briefly touched the terrible reality of insanity and, having glimpsed it, could not resist synthesizing the experience in paint. It is that state of temporary madness —equivalent to what he had just suffered—that Goya reveals in the crowds in these pictures. There is nothing light-hearted about the carnival revelers in *The Burial of the Sardine (page 20),* for instance. The movement of individuals within the mass is grotesque and graceless, and nearly everyone wears a mask—a horrible caricature of human features.

To Goya's contemporaries these works must have come as an interesting surprise. The flat theatrical lighting of the tapestry cartoons has disappeared and with it the smoothness of surface and line that was so characteristic of the early Goya. Now the brushwork has become harsh and jagged, almost feverish, and the compositions are crowded to the bursting point, as if the artist had been trying to cram into these small pictures everything he had left out of his former work.

But this was only the beginning. Goya was still recording only the outer manifestations of madness. He had yet fully to explore the strange images—not quite of this world—that, somehow, his illness freed from his unconscious and brought to the surface of his sensibility. For the moment, now that the worst had passed and he had indulged his long-suppressed desire to exercise his capacity for "caprice and invention," Goya returned to work of a more familiar sort.

In the spring of 1794 Bayeu wrote that his brother-in-law had recovered somewhat and was painting again, "though not with his former tenacity and constancy." He made no comment about any noticeable change in the quality of that work, mostly portraiture and not appreciably different from the commissions Goya had executed prior to his illness.

Goya obviously still hoped he might be freed from his deafness as he had been freed from his paralysis. Feelings of alienation and impotent rage at his suffering, soon to be an integral part of his sensibility, had not yet had time to grow in him. He could still realistically dream of a return to complete normalcy, and he still clung stubbornly to such shreds of his old habits as he could grasp in his new circumstances. Moreover, conditions in Spain had not yet deteriorated to the point where the external world would seem to Goya an extension of his own inner turmoil. But that time was not far off.

By 1794 Prime Minister Floridablanca and his immediate successor, the Count of Aranda, had both been dismissed and the insufferable Godoy, still in his mid-twenties, had been given the post. In quick succession he had been made a Lieutenant General of the Army, Duke of Alcudia and a grandee and member of the Council of State, from which posts he took charge of the nation's destiny. Godoy failed in the first tasks assigned him by his sovereigns, although, in fairness, it is possible that no one could have succeeded. He was unable to rescue the French Royal Family—cousins of Bourbon Charles IV—from the revolutionary guillotines. He was also unable to prevent the onset of the war that the aggressive young French Republic declared on Spain.

On the other hand, this war, in which Spain had the satisfaction of defending the principle of monarchy against the spirit of Enlightenment run riot, did not prove excessively costly—at least in comparison to some of the country's previous military adventures. Spain even had a success or two in Catalonia, which was the war's main battlefield, and she concluded a promising defensive alliance with Great Britain. Despite the fact that Spain was forced to sue for peace (she surrendered her half of the Caribbean island of Santo Domingo to France) the war was short, losses were low and it seemed, at least in court circles, that the good fight had been fought. It even appeared to have had certain internal benefits. The ministries were purged of the liberal officials who had won their places during the reign of Charles III; they were replaced by bureaucrats whose loyalties to the monarchy were absolute and whose devotion to the persons of Charles IV and Maria Luisa was utterly secure. On the whole, Their Highnesses were well pleased by their young protégé, and they rewarded Godoy with yet another title, "Prince of the Peace."

Unconcern with the increasingly dangerous situation in Europe was apparently shared by Goya as well as by everyone else in Madrid, and the quality of upper-class existence remained remarkably unchanged. One small measure of this unconcern about the nation's political future was the decision by the leading aristocratic family to engage a well-known painter to do their portraits in oils. The name of the family was Alba; the name of the painter was Francisco Goya.

The Duke and Duchess of Alba were undoubtedly known to Goya before 1795. There is, in fact, some reason to believe that Goya may have included the Duchess in one or two of his tapestry cartoons, perhaps even among some of the figures who populate the decorative paintings he did for the Duchess of Osuna's palace. This would have been dangerous, considering the rivalry between the two women, but it was the kind of small, childishly rebellious joke the painter enjoyed. Nor does the use of the Duchess as a figure in the cartoons presuppose any intimacy between the painter and herself. She was a legendary beauty whose features were well known to every man about Madrid.

In any case, the relationship between Goya and the highborn lady did not truly flourish until he began frequenting her new palace, in the heart of Madrid, in the summer of 1795. The portrait he painted of her husband (*page 76*) suggests the reason why Goya, along with other robust, distinctly masculine types, was interesting to the Duchess. The Duke, as Goya portrayed him, was a slender, elegant man, far wearier than he should have been at the age of 39. He stands near a harpsichord, a score by Haydn (with whom he corresponded) clutched in his hand to symbolize the one passion of his life, music. Shy, withdrawn, sensitive, the antithesis of the ideal Spanish male, he was quite unlike those hearty, haughty and highly independent men who had dominated the Alba line for centuries and whose style set the standards the Duchess herself adopted and admired in others. She had married when she was 13 and her husband was only 19, and it quickly became clear to her that the match was unsatisfactory. By the time she was in her early twenties she had become, for many reasons, the most famously controversial woman in Spain.

Of her beauty there is no doubt. "The Duchess of Alba has not a hair on her head that does not provoke desire," a French traveler wrote.

"When she passes everyone looks from their windows and even children leave their games to look at her." Poets sang:

> . . . *the glory*
> *of your beauty; the potent caress*
> *of your eyes provoking forever . . .*

and they spoke, too, of

> *those sparkling eyes of yours*
> *and that mouth, all smiles . . .*

Her disdain of convention was equally famous, although her motives were surely mixed. The record of her charitable activities is extensive, and there was a sincerity about them that transcends the spirit of *noblesse oblige*. There is no doubt that her embrace of majaism also went beyond the self-titillating gestures of her peers. For her, the style and manner of the lower classes were not merely a costumed charade, but a way of expressing her active contempt for the idle vapidity of her own class.

But the words of a contemporary must also be borne in mind. "She had received no education, nor heard good precepts, nor read good books nor seen but bad examples." She was by no means a self-conscious, guilt-ridden aristocrat attempting to ingratiate herself with the downtrodden. Neither was she any amateur social theorist basing her behavior on some abstract notion of democratic justice. Essentially she was a high-spirited, intellectually and emotionally undisciplined woman in constant search of relief from boredom and as capable of finding that relief in cruelty as she was in kindness. Indeed, the two were often inextricably mixed in her behavior. One of her constant companions, for example, was a little Negro girl, Maria de la Luz, whom she had informally adopted. She loved the child, but treated her more like an exotic household pet than a daughter. Another member of her entourage was a lame, stuttering friar, Brother Basil, who was undoubtedly incapable of performing even the most minor religious functions and whose presence in the Alba household represented an act of mercy on the Duchess' part. The good father earned his keep by serving as the butt of an endless series of jokes and pranks played on him by the Duchess and her friends. She was fully capable of exhibiting her cruel sense of comedy with strangers as well. Encountering a young seminarian one day when she was out for a stroll, she pretended poverty and encouraged him to take her to a café where she consumed quantities of food beyond his means to pay. The proprietor, at her whispered behest, insisted that the youth pay his bill with his trousers. Nothing dampened the student's ardor, however, and he was encouraged to visit the Duchess the next day at her palace. Assuming that the Duchess was merely a serving girl, he presented himself confidently and suddenly found himself in the midst of a glittering gathering where his misadventure of the previous day was recounted to the great glee of everyone—and to his intense embarrassment.

The Duchess also preoccupied herself with the intrigues of love—her affairs were many and short-lived—and with the pursuit of two great social rivalries with the Duchess of Osuna and with Queen Maria Luisa. Alba's rivalry with Osuna was a thing of pin pricks and needle thrusts. At one moment the subject of their antagonism would be musical, and their partisanship would quickly divide Madrid society into warring groups devoted to Gluck or Piccini or Lully. At another time matadors would provide the metaphor for their rivalry, one choosing Rodrigo Costillares as champion and lover, the other Pedro Romero. In the course of the battle of the bullfighters, Tomás Yriarte wearily reported, "There is no other talk to be heard from the time one gets up in the morning until he goes to bed at night."

The contest between the Duchess and Maria Luisa was a more serious matter. It began with a lover who moved from the latter's bed to the former's. (This was in the days prior to the Queen's conception of her grand passion for Godoy.) The fellow brought with him a gold box set with diamonds that Maria Luisa had given him. He presented it to the Duchess in exchange for a ring, which, in a mysterious turn, ended up on Maria Luisa's hand. Not to be outdone, the Duchess gave the gold box to her hairdresser, who also served Maria Luisa. He kept pomade in it and was enjoined to carry it whenever he set the royal coiffure.

Most of the time the battle was waged at the level of a catfight, but the Duchess came to believe that two fires that almost destroyed her new palace were set by agents of the Queen. This charge was never proved, but it is clear that Her Majesty took the game more seriously than her younger and more beautiful rival. When the Queen's irritation became insupportable, she ordered the Duchess banished from court. This caused little hardship; the Duchess would simply retire to her country estate at Sanlúcar de Barrameda, near Cádiz, usually taking a lover along to help her fill the empty hours. In a little more than a year, Goya would make that journey.

Goya annotated his visit, during the fall and winter of 1796-1797, to the Duchess of Alba's Andalusian estate near Sanlúcar de Barrameda, with sketches of unexpectedly lighthearted gaiety. In the drawing above he portrayed the arrogant Duchess in a rare tender mood, cuddling Maria de la Luz, her little Negro favorite.

In 1795, however, his relationship with the Duchess was no more intense than it was with many of his other sitters. Indeed, it speaks well for Goya's diplomatic talents that he could place himself in the middle of the crossfire between the Queen, the Duchess of Osuna and the Duchess of Alba and emerge unscathed, able to go on painting for all of them.

There is some reason to believe that the Duchess made the first move in their affair. In August 1795, while Goya was still at work on her husband's portrait, she appeared at his studio. He wrote Zapater that she had come so that he might "paint her face, and she went out with it painted, which I definitely like better than painting on canvas." He added, however, that she was to come again and that he would then paint her in full length.

The result is a brilliant portrait of her in a gold-trimmed white lace dress set off by a wide vermilion sash and two bright ribbons, and with a shaggy miniature white poodle at her feet *(page 66)*. She is posed on a sandy bluff overlooking a distant landscape. Her small mouth is drawn up in a tight bow; there is an imperious look to her eyes, and she points toward the ground with her right hand, almost as if she were ordering someone to kneel before her. Her pride and her beauty are undeniable. But they exist in a void that she seems to be trying to fill by an act of will. One can imagine a tiny foot stamping in anger if her commanding gesture is not instantly obeyed. It is through such a revealing psychological gesture—an arrogant act of command—that Goya has made almost palpable the Duchess' inability to assuage her loneliness or order her emotional emptiness to be filled.

The secret loneliness of Doña Maria Teresa Cayetana de Silva, 13th Duchess of Alba, was something Goya, cut off from much of life by his deafness and by his growing celebrity, could now comprehend with a new sensitivity. He had, mindful of his position, stopped socializing in the cafés and cantinas. Illness and advancing age—he was almost 50— had given him a new awareness of his own mortality. It was at this time, too, that his first and most demanding colleague, Francisco Bayeu, died. Despite the ambiguities of their relationship, Goya felt the loss keenly. The closest link to his earliest days as an artist was now broken. Goya at this time was working on a new portrait of Bayeu, modeled partly on one he had painted from life some years earlier, but the new work was somehow more sensitively aware of the wounds, the sufferings that an artist like Bayeu—one who never fully frees his talents from the constraints of rules and fashions—must endure. Standing on the brink of the artistic breakthrough that Bayeu could never make, Goya painted with a wonderful sympathy and, with symbolic rightness, he left the work unfinished.

And now, too late, he received the most coveted academic appointment in the world of Spanish art. He was asked to succeed his brother-in-law as Director of Painting at the Royal Academy of San Fernando. Hoping, as he said, for some "mitigation of his ills" and unable to refuse a post of such high distinction, Goya accepted the job. But unable to teach, too deaf even to make sense of the Academy's deliberations, he attended no meetings. Two years later, he resigned and was appointed, by acclamation, Honorary Director of Painting.

Meantime, his relationship with the Albas ripened most satisfactorily. When he finished the portraits, he almost immediately did two charming little pictures of everyday life in their palace. He was now, obviously, a familiar figure in this sumptuous household, and it is easy to understand why. The remnants of his old ambition undoubtedly impelled him, but other factors were equally persuasive. Aging, lonely, disturbed mentally, he needed the Duchess' friendship to help restore his faith in himself and in his ability to connect with others. It was proof that his other powers had not failed along with his hearing.

It is almost certain that the Duchess was somewhat less passionate in her concern for him. He was, of course, one of Madrid's most interesting people and, despite his infirmity, something of a social prize. His presence in her home undoubtedly represented a minor victory in her competition with the Queen and the Duchess of Osuna, proof that she could command the attentions of an artist long associated with them. Finally, there is Goya's deafness to consider. The Duchess' attraction to physical or psychological cripples—remember Brother Basil—is well documented and simply explained. They were easy to dominate, and their loyalty and gratitude could usually be commanded with ease.

And so a relationship long misunderstood as a grand passion gradually —even hesitantly—developed out of mutual and probably unexpressed needs. It did not reach a peak until the Duke's frail health finally failed

Working from a sketch made at Sanlúcar, Goya painted this episodic little picture of his hostess, posed characteristically as an accomplished flirt. Here, she uses all the weapons of flirtation—mantilla, fan, eyes and twirling grace—on a beau who resembles Goya in profile, but who appears some 30 years younger than the artist was at the time he knew the Duchess.

him completely in June 1796. The Duchess retired to her estate at Sanlúcar for a year of mourning. It was there that Goya later joined her, and it was there, in a land of stark beauty and wildly contrasting seasonal moods, that a sexual consummation was, if ever, attained.

About that, no one is absolutely certain. Indeed only three things are definitely known about the period when Goya and the Duchess were at Sanlúcar. The first is that the Duchess drafted her will there, leaving most of her vast estate to servants and friends, and including Goya's son, Xavier, among the beneficiaries (he was to receive 10 reales per day in perpetuity). We also know that Goya filled a small notebook with sketches and painted another full-length portrait of the Duchess.

This portrait (page 67) is very similar in pose and mood to the one he executed in 1795, except that the Duchess wears black, perhaps in mourning for her late husband, and that the fingers of her left hand are adorned with two rings, on one of which is inscribed "Alba" and on the other "Goya." The message of the rings is less clear than one might suppose. It was not a public proclamation of love, for Goya never exhibited the painting, keeping it in his home for the rest of his life. It is even possible that he painted in the names at some later time. But there is yet another tantalizing clue. In the sand, facing the Duchess, Goya wrote his name again. A recent cleaning of the picture has revealed that, preceding his name in the sand, Goya had added the word *solo*—"only Goya."

Whether or not Goya and the Duchess were ever lovers—and one inclines to believe that they were—the few surviving pages of the notebook that Goya filled while he was a guest at Sanlúcar testify to an atmosphere both idle and idyllic. Done in India ink wash, the 12 sketches depict women in various, casually erotic moods. The Duchess was clearly the model for three of them, and among the others are two nude studies not definitely identifiable as the Duchess. None of Goya's work carries less emotional charge than these drawings, so lightly tossed off, so clearly the work of an artist at happy rest and finding easy occupation for a hand unable to abandon the hard-working habits of a lifetime. They are testimony to the few moments of completely untroubled repose the artist had ever known. And they suggest, although they cannot be said to prove, that for the most part Goya's relationship with the Duchess was at first relatively informal and uncomplicated; there is no hint of love's agony here.

The mood, of course, could not last. Goya could not long accept so casual a liaison, could not resist the temptation to make something deeper, more permanent of it. But he misread his partner, who had never kept a lover for long and was incapable of anything but a superficial relationship with a man. How or when the idyll at Sanlúcar ended is unknown, though some of Goya's later sketches and engravings suggest the Duchess may deliberately have introduced a rival into her household while Goya was still present. In any case, he left.

Nursing love's wounds, Goya was in no hurry to return to Madrid. Before he made his way back to the capital he probably executed—in some haste—three religious paintings for the Santa Cueva (Holy Grotto) in Cádiz, and he apparently stopped off in Seville long enough to do some portraits of saints for a church there. Intense work was obviously what he needed. A friend, the art historian Ceán Bermúdez, recorded the way in which Goya worked on one of the religious subjects. There is in Seville a renowned statue of St. Jerome by Michelangelo's contemporary, Torrigiano. Goya evidently thought it would serve as an excellent model for his portrait of that saint. "In our presence," Bermúdez wrote, "he examined it, climbing up to the grotto in which it stands on two separate occasions, each time remaining there for more than an hour and a quarter." Free imagination seemed to desert Goya when he executed many of his religious works; they often owe something to a previous artist's conception. While that is easily explicable in a young man, it seems strange at this late date, when Goya was at the height of his powers. Why this lack of originality? Did he regard the subject as unworthy of his highest imaginative efforts? Or, conversely, was he so impressed by this church commission that he dared not trust his own vision? Or did he know, by this time, that his unfettered brush was simply too powerful to render conventionally pious works? It is impossible to say, but the problem is a sign of the growing complexity of his artistic personality.

When he finished in Seville, Goya skirted Madrid to make a brief stop in Saragossa. The city was now strange to him. He even found his friendship with Martín Zapater had deteriorated to a point beyond rescue. Zapater's heirs, when they published the Goya correspondence many years later, perhaps shed some light on this when they described the artist's life style: "Flattered by fortune, the painter was living in an atmosphere that was far from pure, and which must have intoxicated him. . . ." Goya tried to repair the friendship, for, after all, Zapater was a link with his past, older and no less strong than Bayeu had been. He painted his friend's portrait again, but the gesture was too little and too late. Within a few years their correspondence petered out completely.

Goya plunged into work the minute he returned to Madrid. And he found a new patron. The most important, though perhaps not the finest paintings of this self-imposed sentence to hard labor were done for Godoy. The Prince of the Peace had by this time managed to maneuver his country into another war—this time with its erstwhile ally, England—and when Goya set to work, the Spanish navy was trying to recover from a frightful mauling, and the English had set up a blockade of Cádiz. The war was to drag on for 12 years, though at relatively small cost to Spain, its enemy being principally preoccupied with the Napoleonic threat during most of that time.

The war was of less concern to Godoy, however, than the possibility of securing his station in life with a suitable marriage. To bed with royalty was his ambition, and he had dared to dream the impossible dream— a match with the granddaughter of Louis XVI of France. When revolution rendered that liaison out of the question he turned closer to home, fastening upon the young cousin of the King and Queen, the Countess of Chinchón. She was the sweetly innocent daughter of the Infante Don Luis, whom Goya had painted when she was a child (page 70). The cuckolded King was as ignorant of Godoy's true motives as he was of his past transgressions with the Queen, who had already borne a child by Godoy—it was an open secret. For her part, the Queen was desperately unhappy over an affair Godoy was having with one Josefa Tudo, allegedly the daughter of a concierge and, by blessing his marriage to the countess, she hoped to reassert her control over him—or at least to keep him from straying significantly beyond the range of the Royal Family.

And so it was done. Godoy immediately embarked on plans to refurbish one of his two palaces in Madrid, rendering it suitable for a bride of the countess' rank and in keeping with his own advanced position in society. Of course, Spain's leading artist must do some decorations for it.

Goya may not have been overly impressed with the honor. But he accepted the work. He executed three handsome medallions for the entrance way—representing *Commerce*, *Agriculture* and *Industry*—and for the library he created a pair of large allegories—*Spain, Time and History* and *The Allegory of Poetry*. It is also possible that for this most unlikely of patrons Goya painted, around 1800, his most famous, most debated works, *The Clothed Maja* and *The Naked Maja (pages 68-69)*.

If this dating of these works is correct, it would go far toward sensibly settling, once and for all, the controversy as to whether they do or do not represent the Duchess of Alba. The one incontrovertible fact about the *Majas* is that they were owned by Godoy—they are first mentioned in the inventory of his estate that was made on January 1, 1808, where they are titled *Gypsy Clothed* and *Gypsy Nude*. It is possible that they were painted on his commission, for he was both powerful enough and interested enough in the subject to defy the ancient ban on nudes. (His licentiousness was endless; as Prime Minister he was notorious for scheduling interviews with attractive female petitioners at night, and they were often seen leaving his palace office in a disheveled state.) Finally, there is a sizable and respectable, though not necessarily majority view among scholars that the technique of the *Majas* matches the technique Goya exhibited in other paintings at this time. No one, of course, believes that they are portraits of the Duchess. But if Goya did paint them at this time is it not possible that with the memory of the Duchess so fresh in his mind he hired a model who resembled her? Is it not possible that in painting this double he may have unconsciously emphasized her likeness to the Duchess? Might not he even have done so with conscious malice, enjoying the thought of her being mistaken for this shamelessly seductive, shamelessly naked woman in the home of the loathsome Godoy? It is more than possible, for such acts of sly duplicity were not unknown to him and, as we shall see, Goya had displayed his embittered opinion of the Duchess' character far more publicly than this. In any case, it is the most reasonable answer to a tantalizing enigma.

The problem of the *Majas* will never be solved to everyone's total satisfaction, but of the main thrust of Goya's career at this point there can be little doubt. He had known the edge of madness, he had seen close-up the decadence of the court and heard the far-off rumble of revolutionary ideas and guns. He could see that in Spain, as elsewhere, the Age of Reason was drawing to a close.

He resisted acknowledgment of this truth, which was dreadful to him, and that resistance took two forms. He hastened to make portraits of his friends, intellectual mentors and sponsors who had so bravely attempted to introduce the Enlightenment to Spain. In 1797-1798 he painted, among others, the poet Juan Antonio Meléndez Valdés and the connoisseur Bernardo Yriarte—for whom he had painted his "popular diversions." The eminent physician, Dr. Peral, sat for him and so did Spain's Minister of Justice, Jovellanos—himself only a few years away from exile. They are all wonderful portraits—strong, sober, thoughtful, and above all, respectful; they are almost epitaphs.

It was through Jovellanos' influence that Goya received one of his great commissions of the period—frescoes for the little church of San Antonio de la Florida in Madrid *(pages 89-95)*. At first glance it may not have seemed to Goya a very promising place to decorate. Its dome is cramped; the walls to be decorated are broken into oddly dimensioned shapes. And yet here in a poor, outlying district Goya created paintings that were his most significant departure from all that had preceded. The subject was St. Anthony of Padua, a very popular figure among the Spanish people, performing his most famous miracle, raising a dead man to life to exonerate his father from a false accusation of murder. The saint stands surrounded by a motley assemblage of *majas,* workers, beggars and thieves. There is, for once, no conventional piety here, no reworkings of the standard devotional forms. Instead, what Goya painted is a magnificent statement of humanism, the belief in and love of the common man, one of the great themes of enlightened thought. The people are awed by the saint and his miracle, but they press around him curious, familiar and wondrously alive and natural. For once Goya had united the world of the flesh with the world of the spirit, for once his enigmatic religious convictions and his often unexpressed love of ordinary humankind are openly and simultaneously stated in one exultant work.

But it is not a beginning, it is an ending. For while he painted his frescoes, he was also working on a series of pictures that delved into the dark world of witchcraft. It was a fashionable subject in Madrid and in Europe and hence a measure of the dwindling force of rationalism. The Osuna family bought six small studies of supernatural subjects from Goya. Two of the paintings are simply illustrations of popular plays of the time, which dealt with witches, hobgoblins and the like. All are painted in a sardonic, mocking spirit, with firm lines and bright colors *(pages 22-23)*. The artist was obviously attracted to his subject—he painted well and carefully, but he was not yet ready to surrender himself to it completely. His stance is rather that of the objective reporter.

This was something of a pose, a brave assertion of a skeptical spirit in the face of compelling, subjective evidence that rationalism was beginning to fail him as well as his society. In his pocket he was now carrying another notebook. Unlike the sensual anecdotes he had sketched at Sanlúcar, now he set out to satirize, in the spirit of healthy, reasonable chastisement, "human error and folly." Another year would pass before he would publish the results (as etchings), and in that time he would see "the accent of incurable night" settle upon his little drawings, see his satire assume nightmarish form. It surprised him—he did not know all this was in him. But he was powerless to stop it from emerging.

In 1798, while he was decorating the church of San Antonio de la Florida *(pages 88-95)*, Goya painted this portrait of Asensio Juliá, inscribing it "Goya, to his friend Asensio." Juliá's loose coverall, the scaffolding and paint pots suggest that he acted as Goya's assistant while the master created his superb frescoes. A disciple, and perhaps the only pupil of Goya, Juliá later specialized in scenes of the Peninsular War and taught at the Royal Academy of San Fernando.

The Sleep of Reason

Spanish society in the late 18th Century, influenced as it was by the spirit of the Enlightenment, considered reason the guiding force of man; human behavior and political order were directly tied to it. Yet Goya, like many of his countrymen, could see all around him that reason had never prevailed; Spanish life was shot through with corruption, the royal court was the gathering place of indifferent, privileged boors. Against this background, Goya began to explore, through etchings, the dark underside of this pretentious world. His first effort was a series of 80 prints, the *Caprichos* (caprices), published in 1799. Before he left for France in 1824 to live out his last years in Bordeaux, he completed an even more personal series, the *Disparates* (follies) or *Proverbios* (proverbs), which was never published in his lifetime. With these works, Goya took etching—and social comment—to heights seldom reached before or since.

The *Caprichos* were completed following a crippling illness, which carried Goya to the brink of death and left him wasted and totally deaf. In them, Goya revealed some of his own anxieties—those of a man stricken by a cruel physical handicap. But, more important, he preferred devastatingly cogent satires that laid bare the sources of folly: vanity, lechery, superstition, excessive pride, self-deception. In his captions for the *Caprichos,* printed below the engravings on the following pages, Goya also demonstrates his gift for pungent writing.

This engraving from the *Caprichos* provides the theme for the entire work: when man allows his reason to sleep, the creatures of the irrational world control his life; only with the awakening of reason, will these hobgoblins finally disappear.

El sueño de la razon produce monstruos.   The sleep of reason produces monsters.

Imagination abandoned by reason produces impossible monsters: united with her, she is the mother of the arts and the source of their wonders.

109

El de la rollona   Nanny's boy

Negligence, tolerance and spoiling make children capricious, naughty,
vain, greedy, lazy and insufferable. They grow up and yet remain
childish. Thus is nanny's little boy.

Nadie se conoce   Nobody knows himself

The world is a masquerade. Face, dress and voice, all are false.
All wish to appear what they are not; all deceive and do not even
know themselves.

Todos caerán   All will fall

And those who are about to fall will not take warning from the example
of those who have fallen! But nothing can be done about it: all will fall.

Qual la descañonan!   How they pluck her!

Hens, i.e., pretty lasses, also encounter birds of prey to pluck them, and
that is why the saying goes: you'll get as good as you give.

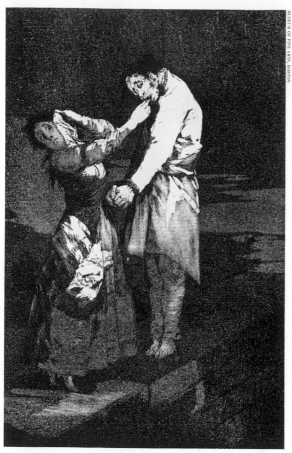

A caza de dientes   Out hunting for teeth

The teeth of a hanged man are very efficacious for sorceries;
without this ingredient there is not much you can do. What a pity
the common people should believe such nonsense.

Que sacrificio!   What a sacrifice!

That's how things are! The fiancé is not very attractive, but he is rich,
and at the cost of the freedom of an unhappy girl, the security of a
hungry family is acquired. It is the way of the world.

Hasta la muerte   Until death

She is quite right to make herself look pretty. It is her 75th brithday,
and her little girl friends are coming to see her.

Miren que grabes!   Look how solemn they are!

The print shows that these are two witches of means and position
who have gone out to take a little exercise on horseback.

111

Aguarda que te unten   Wait until you've been anointed

He has been sent out on an important errand and wants to go off
half-anointed. Even among the witches, some are hare-brained,
impetuous, madcap, without a scrap of judgment. It's the
same the world over.

Linda maestra!   Pretty teacher!

The broom is one of the most necessary implements for witches;
for besides being great sweepers, as the stories tell, they
may be able to change the broom into a fast mule and go with it
where the devil cannot reach them.

No te escaparas   You will not escape
She who wants to be caught never escapes.

No hay quien nos desate?   Can't anyone untie us?
A man and a woman tied together with ropes, struggling to get loose
and crying out to be untied quickly? Either I am mistaken, or they are
two people who have been forced to marry.

Ya es hora   It is time

Then, when dawn threatens, each one goes on his way. Witches, hobgoblins, apparitions and
phantoms. It is a good thing that these creatures do not allow themselves to be seen except by night and
when it is dark! Nobody has been able to find out where they shut themselves up and hide during the
day. If anyone could catch a denful of hobgoblins and were to show it in a cage at 10 o'clock in the
morning in the Puerta del Sol, he would need no other inheritance.

OVERLEAF: Some close-ups of faces seen in the *Caprichos.*

Disparate Ridiculo   Ridiculous Folly
To go amongst the branches, that is, to talk through one's hat.

Chilling Scenes from a Private Hell

Students and admirers of Goya have puzzled over one of his last series of engravings since they were first published in 1864, some 36 years after his death. Goya had worked on these plates as an elderly man and had stored them in Madrid unnumbered, unpublished and unexplained. What Goya intended to call this work is not even certain; some think it was to be the *Sueños* (dreams), a name that the nightmare quality of the engravings would bear out. But today they are known both as the *Disparates* (follies) and *Proverbios* (proverbs), the title with which they were first published. On the following pages, the engravings are coupled with the contemporary sayings most closely associated with them. These proverbs evidence the connection between Goya's dreamlike etchings and the everyday life of his time.

But these engravings transcend mere illustrations of folk sayings. What more do they mean, these weird glimpses into an aging master's mind? There is no exact answer. With the *Disparates* Goya takes his commentary on human existence to a level of fantasy that soars beyond that of the *Caprichos*. Here Goya draws his subjects from the distorted world of dreams and nightmares, a hallucinatory realm peopled by half-humans and strange creatures acting out scenes against the black background of night. Goya draws the fantastic with such a sure hand, and with such ghostly ambience, that the etchings are like photographs sent back from a place few men have ever imagined. Only in the famous "Black Paintings" *(pages 173-185)* does the artist exceed the *Disparates* in offering intimate views of his intensely private world.

116

Disparate Volante   Flying Folly
Renounce the friend who covers you with his wings and bites you with his beak.

Disparate Desordenado   Disorderly Folly, also known as *Disparate Matrimonial*   Matrimonial Folly
She who is ill-wed never misses a chance to say so.

El Caballo Raptor   The horse as abductor
A woman and a horse, let someone else master them.

La Lealtad   Loyalty
He who does not like you will defame you in jest.

118

Modo de Volar   A way of flying

Where there's a will there's a way.

Disparate puntual   Precarious folly

Dancing on a slack rope, i.e., skating on thin ice.

119

21

VI

Los Caprichos: Society Unmasked

Goya's mood in 1797 was more complicated than he realized. He had returned from his interlude with the Duchess of Alba at Sanlúcar dazzled
—and perhaps somewhat dazed—by what he had seen and what he
had felt. He had been exposed to what one biographer describes as "a
world of desire, jealousy, coquetry, feminine intimacy and utter abandon." Back in Madrid he had begun a new sketchbook, larger and
thicker than the one he filled at Sanlúcar and radically different from it
in tone. The portrayals of the Duchess and her female attendants in
the first set of drawings are, if anything, celebrations of female grace
and beauty. In the Madrid sketches, while women are often beautiful,
they have entered the world; these are women in contact with men
and subject to debauchery and depravity. In this sketchbook Goya begins to make use of caricature, to present the human figure distorted
by appetites and passions "in order to convey," as art historian José
López-Rey says, "the crumbling of rationality under a weighty fabric
of social custom." But Goya's stance is optimistic—he believes that
man is capable of rising above vanity and venality, capable of attaining
that greatness of spirit which all rational moralists believe to be potentially within reach. At this point, whatever hurts Goya has suffered at
the hands of the Duchess of Alba, whatever dismay he feels about the de-
clining quality of life in the Spanish court, seem to him expressible
and curable through his art.

Goya was, however, a brooder, not an intellectual. We have seen
that almost two years had passed before he fully discharged the emotions created by his previous illness by painting his series of "popular
diversions." And Goya was never anything but resistant to the self-con-
sciously intellectual approach to the creation of art. Now, "leaving his
usual studio," as one of his friends wrote, "he rented a kind of attic at
the corner of the street of San Bernardino in which he put a table and
some boards." It was to this garret that he retreated, when time allowed, to bend over the blank copper plates on which he etched. It
was there, in isolation, that he slowly allowed images from his unconscious—from the unconscious of the entire race—to emerge and form

themselves on the plates into strange, previously unseen patterns. It was there that he created his *Caprichos (pages 109-115).*

The work was arduous—80 finished plates and innumerable trial proofs were created in the course of two years, and Goya paid very careful attention to the details of his art, employing the techniques of both aquatint and dry point to emphasize certain subtleties. His stress in the early plates is largely on the inconstancy of woman, her selfishness and deceitfulness, her capacity for sexual depravity. There can be little doubt as to which woman in particular inspired these thoughts; indeed, the features of the Duchess of Alba are quite clearly recognizable in at least four etchings. Goya also takes a peculiar delight in showing a cruel justice meted out to women who toy lightly with love. Early in the *Caprichos* such females are depicted raped, imprisoned, being led to the whipping post. There is little doubt that Goya was having delayed revenge on the Duchess as he scratched away with his etching tools.

On the other hand, it must not be supposed that he held his own sex in any higher regard. One of his themes was the hypocrisy of opposing evil with more evil, and he is careful to show men who are unfortunately susceptible to feminine wiles, yet also excessively eager to inflict sadistic punishment on the wicked. Moreover, he distributes commission of the seven deadly sins impartially to both sexes—there is complete equality when it comes to depicting the practitioners of lust, avarice and the rest of the classic catalogue.

As Goya etched, however, calm reason began to wither. The suppressed passions of a lifetime, the rages, hatreds, injuries he had sustained or observed over the years were summoned up, and they began to shape his work. Under their pressure, the human image grew more and more distorted until, in the 37th plate, it was abandoned. In this and in the five plates that immediately follow, men are converted into asses, solemnly teaching school, pompously posing for portraits, practicing medicine, earnestly searching genealogies to prove their claims to distinguished ancestry. The 42nd plate restores man to the work. But now he is peculiarly burdened. Two sleepwalkers stumble about, carrying asses on their backs. The braying beasts represent, of course, the weight of man's animalistic stupidities in education, politics and society—unworthy and incapacitating burdens.

With that plate, night closes down completely on the *Caprichos.* Immediately after it Goya inserted a work he had intended as a frontispiece —a self-portrait in which he is shown asleep at his desk *(page 109).* Gleaming-eyed cats crouch nearby, and out of the depths of darkness winged creatures come swooping down on him. Goya's title, *The Sleep of Reason Produces Monsters,* is inscribed on the side of the desk. Thereafter, in almost every plate monsters hover in the air or squat upon the ground. Sometimes they tear at the naked grotesques who have conjured them up, sometimes they carry them off, sometimes they merely sport with them in depraved play.

To each picture, Goya added a caption. But as one writer says of these brief phrases, "He complicated what was already enigmatic by accompanying it with a paraphrase intended for the further confusion of anyone

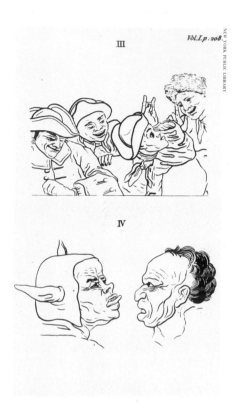

Goya's grotesques derive essentially from his own somber imagination, but he was doubtless familiar with a theory current in his time, which insisted that an individual's moral state affects his physical features. This theory's leading proponent was a Swiss, Johann Kaspar Lavater, who drew the illustrations above for his widely read *Essays on Physiognomy.* In his captions for these drawings, Lavater solemnly pointed out that the middle profile in the group of merry tipplers at top exhibits blatant perversion, and that the kerchiefed woman and the man below display "the last stages of brutal corruption." He cited the woman's porcine nose and bony forehead and the man's slack, degenerate lower jaw. Lavater's preposterous theory suggested that character can change bony structures as well as softer features, and it reflects the idiocies to which a slavish devotion to "pure reason" could lead.

who did not have the key to the riddle." This implies that there was some secret, simple explanation for the later plates of the *Caprichos,* that they perhaps contain some carefully disguised criticism of the court—which was under heavy attack at that time from clandestine pamphleteers. If this is true, however, no one has deciphered the code Goya employed. He had also, however, written somewhat more lengthy texts for his pictures. André Malraux finds that Goya's captions—and these longer commentaries that he jotted down but did not publish—are exclamations of surprise, showing us "Goya's astonishment before figures which are partly strangers to him." In short, working without a commission to guide him and with only himself to please, Goya quite simply lost control of his imagery. He could not confine it to the service of the rational, satirical spirit in which he had begun his enterprise.

The first announcement of the *Caprichos* appeared in the newspaper, *Diario de Madrid,* on Feb. 6, 1799, and, like many another advertisement before and since, it is best described as no more than half-truthful. Goya may have employed one of his learned friends to help draft the piece, for by this time he was aware that he had far exceeded his original intentions, and he may have hoped to forestall at least some of the questions and criticism he anticipated would quickly follow publication. In defense of Goya, it may be said that this notice accurately described his original intent as well as the spirit that could still be discerned in about half the plates of the series. In it, Goya explained that he had "chosen from the multitude of follies and blunders common in every civil society as well as from the vulgar prejudices and lies authorized by custom, ignorance or interest, those that he has thought most suitable matter for ridicule as well as for exercising the artificer's fancy."

Disclaiming any attempt to satirize existing society or particular individuals, Goya suggested that "painting (like poetry) chooses from the universal what it considers suitable to its own ends: it reunites in a single fantastic personage circumstances and characteristics that nature has divided among many. From such a combination, ingeniously arranged, results the kind of successful imitation for which a good artificer deserves the title of inventor and not that of servile copyist."

It all *sounds* rational enough, and some of the etchings in the series lend support to these generalizations and to the supposition that Goya started out with nothing deeper in mind than a light satirical comment on the human condition. That he ended up with something quite different was, naturally, obvious to him.

Still, when Goya saw what he had done, his plates must have been irresistible to him. He had never seen anything like them before and, indeed, neither had the world. To be sure, one can find subjects like his in Gothic art and a statement of some of the themes in the paintings of the Flemish masters of the 15th and 16th Centuries—Bosch and Bruegel in particular. But those Gothic grotesques were never charged with Goya's energy, and the fantastic, hellish landscape of the Flemish paintings is quite different from the world of Goya's etchings.

Goya evidently printed about 300 sets of the *Caprichos,* a considerable undertaking. With 80 plates in the series, the work would involve mak-

Many of the sketches Goya made in Madrid after returning from Sanlúcar form the basis for etchings he included in the *Caprichos.* Disillusioned by the unhappy conclusion of his relationship with the Duchess of Alba, he used her features in such graphic denunciations of women as the one above. Goya emphasized the hussy's cold disdain for the beggar woman in his caption for the *Capricho* etching: "God forgive her: and it was her mother!"

ing some 24,000 perfect impressions, not to mention sheets that were destroyed or damaged in the printing process. They were placed on sale, following the February 6 advertisement in the *Diario,* at a small shop that sold liqueurs and perfumes located in the building in which Goya had lived since 1779 and where he was probably living at the time. Apparently he had been unable to find a bookshop willing to put them on display. Two weeks later Goya placed a second advertisement in the *Gazeta de Madrid,* another newspaper. The price of the *Caprichos* was one ounce of gold, or 320 reales, per set—rather inexpensive considering Goya's eminence. Among his first customers were the Osunas, who purchased four sets of the etchings even before they were offered to the public. But the Osunas were to be among Goya's last customers for the *Caprichos.* During the next four years only 27 sets were sold.

This extraordinary neglect of a work by Spain's leading artist is astonishing. Here was a chance for middle-class art fanciers to own original creations (at about one dollar per print) by the man who was paid thousands by aristocrats. No one really knows why the *Caprichos* sold so badly. It has been suggested—indeed, it is the majority view—that the Inquisition laid its heavy hand on the work, perhaps because of the anticlerical tone of some of the plates. But there is no clear evidence that Goya was ever called before a church tribunal or reprimanded either privately or publicly. Similarly, although the court was especially sensitive to criticism at the time the *Caprichos* went on sale, there is no evidence that the government intervened to suppress what might be construed as attacks on its judicial, educational or legislative procedures. The probability is that it was not on an institutional level that the Spaniards of 1799 rejected the *Caprichos,* but on a personal one. The best explanation for the indifference with which the *Caprichos* were met is that Goya's etching needle pierced too deeply the skins of people of all classes, professions and types. These were satires of behavior that almost everyone would prefer not to think about, much less see in the potent graphic form that Goya had devised. Even John Ruskin, the greatest of the 19th Century English art critics, who could easily have been objective about them, found the *Caprichos* impossible to take; he once set fire to a copy.

Whatever anxiety or disappointment the failure of the *Caprichos* caused Goya, he found a way, in July 1803, of turning a profit on the work. He made a formal offer of all the plates to the King for the Royal Printing Office. In October of that year Goya wrote to the King's minister, Miguel Cayetano Soler, gratefully acknowledging receipt of the royal order of acceptance and expressing thanks for "the pension of 12,-000 reales which His Majesty has been pleased to grant to my son." At the same time he forwarded 240 sets that had been printed and remained unsold. Thus, he had found a way of profitably and honorably disposing of a work that had certainly caused him some financial embarrassment (at retail the material he ceded to the King was worth some 75,000 reales) and may also have brought him social discomfort.

Goya was thankful to be done with the whole business. The *Caprichos* had, in any case, served their most pressing psychological purpose by purging him of the long winter of depression and alienation that had afflicted him in varying degrees and with varying intensity ever since his illness. That he was able to extract material benefit from his disposition of the plates—the pension for Xavier was to finance travel abroad—gave a final fillip to the elimination of a potential danger to his career.

Publication of the *Caprichos* did not, apparently, affect Goya's standing at the court. He was now First Painter to the King, and by September of 1799 he was obliged to discharge the duties of that office on a scale unprecedented for him. The Queen wanted no less than two portraits of herself—one clad in a mantilla, in the style of the other great ladies Goya had painted, the other on her favorite horse, Marcial, which had been a gift from Godoy. Neither was an easy task for Goya, for Her Majesty was about as unpromising a subject as a painter can have—heavy in body and features, double-chinned, thick-lipped, with a broad nose and eyes lacking any hint of feminine softness.

Still, Goya painted her truthfully in both instances, and he did very little to ease the discomfort she experienced while sitting for him. She posed for him at El Escorial, one of the two royal residences in the Guadarrama mountains outside Madrid, and she complained particularly of the torments she underwent in sitting for the equestrian portrait. "I have spent two and a half hours perched up on a platform," she wrote Godoy, "with five or six steps to get up to it, with my hat on, and my cloth stock and dress in order that Goya might proceed." A little later she noted that she had been "very patient . . . I have been roasted for two and a half hours . . . and there is still tomorrow to finish off: God grant that the likeness be as good as we wish." It was, though Marcial did not come off as well, looking, as one scholar commented, like "two halves of different animals juxtaposed."

The Queen, however, did not notice the injustice done her favorite mount. She seems, in fact, to have had little mind of her own in artistic matters, accepting the word of courtiers as to the worthiness of Goya's work. They apparently encouraged her to allow Goya to go ahead with what was to be the greatest of his royal commissions, *The Family of Charles IV (pages 72-75)*. In the spring of 1800 the Queen reluctantly consented to the project. From the Aranjuez Palace she wrote Godoy, "If Goya can paint our picture there [in Madrid], doing it well, and obtaining a good likeness, so much the better, since that will free us from bother; but, if it does not come out well there, let him come here, much as it vexes us." By June, probably as much to his displeasure as it was to Their Majesties, Goya was again in the royal presence, sketching in oil the 12 members of the Royal Family who were included in the work. A 13th figure is perhaps the future bride of Prince Ferdinand. She was painted with her head turned aside, since a match had not yet been made.

The work was completed a year later. It was the last painting Goya did of the Royal Family on their commission, even though his salary as First Painter never ceased. There are several explanations for his estrangement from the court. One is that when Ferdinand finally took his first wife, the Princess of Naples, Goya refused to paint her features into the large family portrait, since he loathed retouching. It is also possible that the Royal Family took offense at something Goya inserted in the

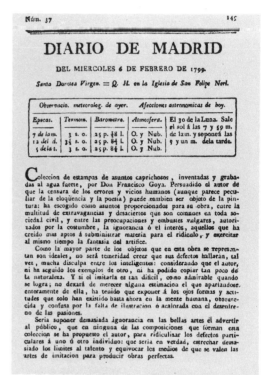

The *Diario de Madrid*, then the major daily Spanish newspaper, printed Goya's advertisement for his series of etchings, the *Caprichos*, on its front page for February 6, 1799. Although this was not an unusual position for such announcements in other journals of the period, the *Diario's* leading article was whatever the editor considered most interesting—sometimes an official announcement, sometimes a satirical poem —and he obviously thought the *Caprichos'* publication was big news. The four-page sheet, unlike its biased and rather prosy competitors, tried to cover Madrid's news, mirroring everything from economic and social reforms to the vagaries of literary and artistic tastes, popular customs and fashion.

Goya dashed off these six oil paintings on wooden panels to celebrate a heroic feat that had all Spain talking. On June 10, 1806, Pedro de Zaldivia, a Franciscan lay brother, singlehandedly captured a notorious bandit known as *El Maragato*. Painted in lively comic-book style, Goya's panels show the young monk wrestling the bandit's gun away from him, throwing him to the ground, shooting at his legs when he tries to run away, then binding his hands while a group of peasants that *El Maragato* had terrorized belatedly threaten the captive.

painting, perhaps one of his typical jokes. Following a recent cleaning of the painting it has been suggested that Goya painted himself into the work not once (he is clearly visible at his easel at the far left) but twice. In one of the pictures that decorate the background wall against which the group is posed, a figure that suspiciously resembles the artist is seen together with two half-nude women, apparently goddesses. It is also possible that the simplest explanation is the best; that the Royal Family was not interested in further encouraging an artist who painted them in such an unflattering, that is to say, truthful light.

By this time Goya had no reason to fear the King and Queen. With that lack of outward fastidiousness about his friends that was so characteristic of him, Goya had drawn closer to Godoy who, after a brief eclipse, was now restored to power. The artist recorded with evident pleasure the fact that he had shared a carriage with the Prime Minister on one occasion and had occupied the time by attempting to teach him the sign language of the deaf. His easy acceptance of Godoy's company and favors does not imply that Goya was ignorant of the man's true nature. Indeed, it seems that Goya's attitude toward himself in this period was summarized by the superb self-portrait *(page 6)* that he executed for the frontispiece of the *Caprichos,* which is of a man shrouded by the accoutrements of fashion—a tall hat, a high stock, a heavy coat collar—but with his mouth turned slightly downward as if in disapproval. His wicked, ironic, yet committed eye is cocked at the world and almost winking. In short, he was a man who saw much, yet revealed only what he chose to of his thoughts and emotions—and then only indirectly.

After the period of hot creativity, which came to an end with the *Caprichos,* Goya had entered upon a long period of canny coolness, of a new preciseness and understatement in his best work, which was once again mostly portraiture. Even before beginning *The Family of Charles IV*—the most spectacular work in this new mode—he was at work on a portrait of Godoy's wife, the Countess of Chinchón, which may well be the greatest of all his portraits *(page 70)*. She sits in a delicate chair, the pure white of her dress in eloquent contrast to the dark and featureless background. Atop the red curls of her hair an absurd little feathered bonnet is perched. She glances to one side, as if too modest to confront the painter—or the viewer—directly, and there is a fineness about her features, a delicacy in her complexion, that one rarely observes in portraits of Spanish ladies of this time, who seem generally to have been of a more robust breed. The brown eyes are sad, empty and innocent. And she is carrying Godoy's child. Goya never spoke more hauntingly of the loneliness of existence than he did in this tragic and beautiful portrait.

Until the outbreak of war with Napoleon's France in 1808, Goya would paint with similar grace and gravity—and perception—on numerous occasions. Most authorities think the male portrait most closely matching the quality of that of the Countess of Chinchón was the one he executed in 1803 of the Count of Fernán-Núñez. That picture, like the royal portraits, approaches open satire. The count assumes a heroic, almost Byronesque pose, a black cape swirled about him, an elegant leg thrust forward, an enormous tricorn hat framing a soft face that belies the strength and formality of the pose. It is the face of a fop who dreamed of power and had to be content with the embassy in London.

At least a dozen portraits that must be regarded almost as highly as this one date from what has been described as a period of "fruitful well-being." Yet, curiously, erratically mixed among the masterpieces are others that are animated only by technical facility, pictures that exhibit neither passion nor penetration. Typical is the portrait of Godoy *(pages 70-71)*, sprawled on a sofa, before a background cluttered with the symbols of war—a remarkably uninteresting picture, especially since it dates from the same period as the Fernán-Núñez portrait.

In short, coolness could easily turn to coldness and indifference. It was no longer possible for Goya to paint badly, but he could paint disinterestedly if his spirit or that of his subject did not move him. In later years Xavier Goya would recall that for his father at this point, "there was nothing left . . . to conquer in painting . . . he knew the magic (an expression he always used) of atmosphere in a picture." Now in his late fifties, he had won all honors, possessed all the wealth he needed and had accepted his deafness. All artistic passion seemingly spent on the *Caprichos,* he gave every evidence of being content to pass his days in a state that must be regarded, for an artist of his energy, as semi-retirement.

Goya recorded no response to the death of the Duchess of Alba in 1802, although Madrid buzzed with rumors, still unproved, that she had been poisoned, possibly by the Queen or even by Godoy. There was an unseemly rush for her property when her will, which had left most of her estate to servants and charity, was invalidated. Goya apparently made no mention of that scandalous scene either. It was at this time that he moved into the grandest house he had yet occupied, a granite-walled affair with a paved porch and courtyard in a fashionable quarter, for which he paid 80,000 reales.

If he suffered any sadness at all during this period of his life, it was over what appears to have been a brief estrangement from his beloved Xavier. The boy had made a good marriage to the daughter of Goya's old and well-to-do friend, Martín de Goicoechea, and Goya invited Xavier and his new wife to live with him and Josefa in their new house. The young couple, however, stayed only six months—apparently mother and daughter-in-law could not get along together. Six months after that, father and son were reconciled, and Goya deeded his house over to Xavier, along with 13,055 reales that represented the profits on some money he had invested in stocks, purchased a decade before. He and Josefa moved into more modest quarters.

So life slipped slowly, serenely by. There is no reason to suppose that Goya would have accomplished anything more significant than a few portraits and perhaps a new series of etchings (he would continue to fill sketchbooks with such odd little figures as cripples observed in the streets). But history intervened with violent insistence. Its instruments were the overreaching Godoy, the inept Spanish Royal Family and Napoleon Bonaparte, Emperor of France. The events they set in train would force Goya out of the lethargy that had lately stolen over him and drive him again to the heights of his talent.

Disasters
of War

In 1808 Goya was 62 years old, a respected and wealthy court painter whose work had ranged from gay tapestry designs to perceptive portraits, stunning murals and powerful etchings. Deaf and growing old, Goya had no reason to believe that some of his most original work was still before him. But political intrigue precipitated on Spain a cruel and unnecessary war—a war that was to present Goya with the backdrop for the work whose vivid truth would help secure him as one of the world's great artists.

Like all wars, this one was originated in a quest for power. The Spanish ruler Charles IV, his perfidious wife Maria Luisa and their loutish eldest son Ferdinand fell to quarreling over who was to rule. In the wings of this squabble was Napoleon, who coveted Spain. Already Napoleon had troops in Spain under the pretext of marching to Portugal. Some royal advisers wanted the foreigners driven out, but Charles had no stomach for battle. He abdicated in favor of his son Ferdinand, who believed that Napoleon would support his regime. Instead, Ferdinand was called to a confrontation with his parents and the French Emperor, and immediately the Spanish ruling family began fighting among themselves. Napoleon, seizing this advantage, took the throne for himself and solidified his troop positions in Madrid, thus setting the stage for a rebellion that would lead to a war lasting six vicious years.

The terror, chaos and grim foreboding that loomed over Spain during the Napoleonic wars of 1808-1814 are symbolized in this painting by Goya. While the frightened populace dashes madly about on the ground, the Colossus, perhaps representing war itself, dominates the sky.

The Colossus, c.1811

129

To govern Spain, Napoleon chose his brother Joseph, who had already proved to be an effective administrator for the Emperor in Naples. But before the choice was made public, Spain rose up against Napoleon.

In Madrid on May 2, 1808, rumors swept the uneasy capital: Napoleon was not going to restore Ferdinand to the throne; the royal family was to be kidnapped and murdered. At the Puerta del Sol near the palace, a large crowd waited to catch a reassuring glimpse of members of the royal family, especially Charles IV's 13-year-old son, who was rumored to be departing for France. The crowd grew restive: was this little lad on his way to assassination? Suddenly, the mood became hostile and the mob surged forward against the French guards. The Spaniards were raked with fusillades of bullets and French re-enforcements were dispatched, including the Mamelukes, the hated Egyptian mercenaries *(at left, in turbans)*. But the mob assault continued, as soldiers were pulled from their horses and attacked with knives and bare hands. It is not known whether Goya witnessed this uprising, but when he commemorated it six years later, he imparted a passionate immediacy that makes it seem as if he had been there.

The Second of May, 1808, in Madrid: the Insurrection against the Mamelukes, 1814

131

The conflict at the Puerta del Sol might not have been enough to start a war, but the next day the French committed a blunder that made war inevitable: they executed, without a trial, all Spaniards believed to have been connected in any way with the uprising. Goya, painting the firing squad six years later, emerged with his most gripping, dramatic masterpiece. The executioners are anonymous soldiers doggedly obeying orders by killing the suspects lined up before them. The focus of the painting is a peasant with arms upraised, his face and posture a mixture of horror, pride and resignation in the face of death.

The volleys from the French firing squads rang throughout Spain. Across the land, fighting *guerrillas* (the word, meaning little wars, was coined at this time) threw themselves on the French soldiers in an impassioned display of nationalistic fury.

Goya's own attitudes toward the war were mixed. Love for Spain and its people emanates from all his work. Yet because he was an admirer of the French Enlightenment, he and many of like mind felt that French rule might be superior to the known inadequacies of Charles IV or Ferdinand. Goya, watching from his studio, recorded the war with his customary objectivity, but the brutality and illogic of it must have strained his sense of reason.

The Third of May, 1808, in Madrid: the Shooting on Principe Pio Mountain, 1814

A portrait of Wellington done in 1812 by Goya shows the haughty, if slightly harried, air of the general who by the brilliant use of his English and Portuguese troops was forcing Napoleon's downfall in Spain.

Tristes presentimientos de lo que ha de acontecer.   Gloomy presentiments of things to come.

A kneeling man, his clothing torn, his eyes lifted toward the heavens, is the first etching in Goya's "Disasters," providing dark hints of what is to follow.

The Disasters of War

Before Goya, artists often showed war as a heroic, ennobling act of man; on huge canvases, soldiers marched off to martial strains leaving behind cheering populations and adoring ladies. Victory was the attainable goddess; honor, the glorifying force. Goya changed all that. He painted—and drew—war as it is, honored by isolated acts of heroism, but more often an inferno that can brutalize man to the point where he commits acts against his fellow beings that exceed the most gruesome imaginings.

Goya traveled through Spain sketching what he saw and felt, but it would have been difficult for him to romanticize the Peninsular War even if he had wanted to;

the war was fought by both sides with no quarter given or asked. The French tortured and mutilated their prisoners, chopping off limbs and organs even after the men were dead. The Spaniards reacted in kind, hacking up the bodies of the enemy and subjecting captives to long agonizing deaths. Hunger, deprivation and misery ravaged the land. From his sketches Goya was to create a devastating series of etchings with eloquent and moving titles. The entire collection, published after Goya's death as *The Disasters of War (reproduced above and following pages with Goya's own original captions in Spanish and in English translations),* is a profound indictment of war and the atrocities that have always flowed in its wake.

137

Que Valor!   What Courage!

One of the few times in the "Disasters" that Goya shows an act of heroism is in this etching of a young woman of Aragon named Agustina, firing a cannon after the male gunners have been killed. The heroine fought beside the men during the French siege of Saragossa.

Ni Por Esas.   And nor do these.

Against the ironically peaceful background of a church, a Spanish mother is dragged away by a French soldier who leaves her baby squalling on the ground. Directly behind them, a soldier grabs a protesting woman, while in the shadows, abject figures crouch and slump.

29

No quieren.   They do not want to.

*The women of Spain, often defenseless against the French soldiers, were frequently the victims of assault and rape. In this stark etching,
Goya shows a soldier attacking a girl, his hands clutching her waist, as an elderly woman, dagger in hand, rises to her defense.*

Enterrar y callar.   Bury them and be silent.

*Corpses, stripped of their clothes by soldiers or peasants and left unburied on a barren hill, are stumbled upon by two of the living
who gag back their revulsion. In powerful scenes like these, Goya shows the bleak, despairing corollary of the presumed glories of war.*

Populacho   The populace

The Spaniards, resentful of the French presence on their soil even before the war began, were murderously revengeful after witnessing the atrocities committed by the foreigners. The bodies of slain French soldiers were subjected to savage indignities that were watched with silent approval.

Tambien esto   And this too

No longer deterred by the protective power of the Inquisition, the French and even some anti-clerical Spaniards pillaged and destroyed many monasteries, turned the monks out and raped the nuns. Goya's notation is a sequel to a previous caption. "Everything has gone wrong."

Grande hazaña! Con muertos!   Wonderful heroism! Against dead men!

The mutilation of corpses was a common sight during this time. Here the severed head, the fettered hands at the ends of arms reaching from nothing toward nowhere, the altered bodies, all hang on the living tree like grotesque ornaments illustrating man's ferocity.

Esto es lo peor!   That is the worst of it!

Churchmen and peasants kneel before a wolf, one of the animal symbols Goya used in his final section of the "Disasters," while the beast writes, "Wretched humanity, the fault is yours." The scene reflects the outrage and disillusionment of the Spanish people in the aftermath of the terrible war.

Murió la verdad.   Truth is dead.

After the war, retrogressive forces again ruled Spain and forced many liberally inclined Spaniards to believe that Truth was indeed dead. At Truth's funeral, presided over by a cleric, Justice (right) hides her eyes in the shadows.

Toward the end of the war, Napoleon was fighting conventional battles in the field against English and Portuguese troops skillfully led by Wellington, while fending off the guerrillas who were striking at unguarded positions. It was too much, and the French retreated across the Pyrenees. As Napoleon tasted defeat in Spain, his Empire began to crumble. Later the exiled Emperor would remark, "The Spanish affair is what killed me."

"The Spanish affair," as he euphemistically called that blood-curdling war, almost killed Spain too. When the war ended in 1814 there was new hope, for a liberal Cortes, or Parliament, was in power. The Cortes, inspired by the quest for freedom that had sparked the French and American Revolutions two and three decades before, supported a forward-looking constitution. Even the arrogant Ferdinand VII, who had been held in France throughout the war, agreed to accept the constitution. But he no more than touched Spanish soil again than he annulled the constitution and immediately began to restore authority to all the old conservative and repressive institutions, like the Inquisition. After a futile effort by the liberals to oppose Ferdinand, the leaders of the Cortes were promised amnesty by the King in return for surrender; as soon as they yielded, the King betrayed them, and they were killed. The constitution was tossed out, and Spain sank back into its familiar state of oppressive lethargy. All that Spain had gained from six years of bloody butchery was a king more backward than their old ruler, Charles IV, and even more insensitive to the plight of his people.

Si resucitará?   Will she rise again?

As the creatures of night stand by, Truth's dying light pierces their dark world, possibly giving hope to the hopeless. Goya's etching poses the question of whether a new spirit of reason can rise from the ashes of irrational war.

Esto es lo verdadero.   This is the truth.

In the etching that concludes the "Disasters" series—a positive footnote to a pessimistic narrative—Goya shows a robust, full-breasted Truth addressing a bearded old farmer, perhaps a suggestion that Spain's ravaged lands may flourish again.

Regozijo

VII

Witness to
a Holocaust

"Politics," as Napoleon Bonaparte was fond of remarking, "is fate," and as one looks back over the regime of Charles IV, the cuckolded king, his nymphomaniacal wife and their depraved Prime Minister, Godoy, it seems remarkable that they were able to stave off fate as long as they did. That they reigned in relative peace and prosperity during this period of political upheaval on the Continent is less a tribute to their nonexistent diplomatic and military skills than to the violent confusions that beset Europe's most threatening force, revolutionary France. That confusion, however, ended late in 1799 when Napoleon staged his coup d'état and proclaimed himself First Consul of the Republic. In five years he would compel the Pope to travel from Rome and stand by submissively as he placed the imperial crown on his own head. But long before that he would gather to himself all the powers of the state, and would be, in fact, dictator of France (and half of Europe). To him, as to so many others who had previously ruled France, the prospect of making the Pyrenees disappear was irresistibly inviting. Considering the quality of the leadership in Spain, it was seemingly an easy task. For all the reforms Charles III had put into practice, Spain was still neither a unified nor a truly modern nation. Spain was still more inviting as a target because many leaders and many among the populace were either naturally predisposed toward France or were heartily tired of the present regime.

The prize was well worth Napoleon's effort. Spain's location gave it control of the Mediterranean and made it a valuable counter to Russia, which had designs on that strategic sea. Spain, of course, also had rich American colonies. Napoleon had hardly begun his tenure as First Consul when he began his attempt to win Spain through subversion, diplomatic pressure, humiliation, threat and every other unwarlike means.

There was nothing particularly subtle in his approach. Bourbon France had treated Bourbon Spain as an ally, an equal partner in its adventures, even though its southern neighbor was manifestly weaker. Napoleon showed no such courtesy. Very simply, he bullied Spain: first into a series of treaties, which made its armed forces mere adjuncts of France's, then into retroceding its Louisiana Territory in North America

Two droll old people click their castanets as they literally dance in the air in this brush drawing titled Mirth, believed to have been done by Goya about 1815. With swift strokes of his ink-laden brush and the lightest veils of wash, Goya created a joyous moment of reality tinged with fantasy.

to France (from which it had been obtained in 1763). This treaty forbade Napoleon from selling Louisiana to any country but Spain, but three years after its signing he blithely sold the territory to the United States (the purchase was negotiated by Thomas Jefferson) and brushed aside Spain's feeble protests. This betrayal represented the most important—though hardly the first—colonial humiliation suffered by Spain; it was the beginning of the end of its position as one of the two dominant powers in the New World, Britain being the other.

It was not until 1805 that Spain fully realized the danger Napoleon posed—and it took the disastrous naval defeat at the hands of the British at Trafalgar, which Spanish ships shared equally with the French, to awaken the nation. Prime Minister Godoy now attempted to withdraw Spain from the French alliance; peace feelers were extended to Britain. Napoleon, alas, had just won his great victories over Prussia and was in no mood to tolerate defections, especially by an ally he regarded as contemptuously as he did Spain. He did not, however, threaten Godoy. Instead he proffered a bribe: join him in mounting a new attack on Portugal, and they would divide that nation three ways—one third for France, one third for Spain and one third for Godoy personally.

The Emperor, as Napoleon now styled himself, had no intention of sharing spoils with Godoy. Instead he was seeking an excuse to peacefully introduce French troops into the Iberian Peninsula in support of his real plan, which was marvelous in its intricacy. Charles IV's eldest son, the Prince of Asturias (later Ferdinand VII) had managed to draw together a motley dissident party, united only by a common hatred of Godoy. Their aim was nothing less than high treason—encompassing, as it did, the murders of the Prime Minister and the Queen, and the deposition of the King. The reprehensible Ferdinand, in every way his parents' child despite his hatred of them, had already written Napoleon begging his "paternal protection" and outlining his plot, in aid of which Napoleon started quietly sending his soldiers into Spain.

Beribboned scion of a hundred kings, Charles IV, pen in hand, confronts Napoleon, the upstart master of Europe, before signing the Treaty of Bayonne on May 5, 1808. The Emperor had summoned the Spanish Royal Family to this meeting to force Charles to resign the Spanish crown, which he had just regained from his son Ferdinand (behind the table). Once the act of abdication was signed, Napoleon coolly arranged for his older brother Joseph to be crowned King of Spain.

There was a temporary setback. Ferdinand's scheme was discovered, and he was tried by his parents for treason. It was only at Napoleon's intercession that a verdict of not guilty was brought in. By this time, however, there were 100,000 French troops in Spain. Wondrously, the Emperor managed to convince both factions that his men were there to protect each against its rival. It was not until the French actually occupied Barcelona and Pamplona that everyone realized they came not as friends but as an occupying force.

The court panicked and decided to flee to the Americas. But they were turned back by a mob at Aranjuez, just a few miles south of Madrid on the road to Cádiz, where a ship awaited them. (Godoy was discovered by the rioters hiding in a rolled-up carpet and was quickly escorted to prison.) Ferdinand caught up with his parents in Aranjuez and urged them to abdicate. In return for this he promised protection from the invaders. Charles accepted the terms, and his son hurried back to Madrid, already occupied by French soldiers under the command of Napoleon's brother-in-law, Joachim Murat. The new King now begged Napoleon to assure him his throne and, in so doing, he definitively placed Spain's fate in the hands of a foreigner. Napoleon had several options: he could grant Ferdinand's request or he could aid Charles, who was now claiming that he had surrendered the throne to his son under duress. In return for assistance to either man, Napoleon could name almost any price. Or, he could simply seize the throne for France—more precisely, for some member of his own family to occupy. It was this plan that most appealed to him, but there was plenty of time to launch it. Meanwhile, in Madrid the ineffable Ferdinand reigned without ruling for several weeks.

It was during the spring of 1808 that Goya edged briefly onto the historical stage. The Royal Academy of San Fernando asked him to paint the new sovereign's portrait for its meeting room. He was able to get only two brief sittings—His Majesty's schedule being understandably crowded. From sketches made at these sittings he undertook to create an equestrian portrait, flattering and facile and not to be compared with the superb standing portrait of the monarch as a faintly moronic, almost gnomish figure that he executed some six years later.

It is a measure of Goya's perseverance that he worked at this portrait from the end of March until early October, during which time its subject was divested of his throne, a foreign usurper placed on it and the whole nation plunged into a civil war bloodier than any civilized country had ever previously known. True to his highly developed instinct for self-preservation, neither in his art nor in conversation did the painter make any comment on this state of affairs. While Spain burned, he painted.

The portrait, he thought, might have been better if his subject had been able to give him more sittings. Unfortunately, His Majesty was called away the day after his second meeting with the painter. Napoleon had invited him to Bayonne, in France, to discuss the Spanish situation. Desperate for the Emperor's backing, the King unsuspectingly crossed the border and found himself confronted not with an offer of aid but with an ultimatum: abdicate in favor of his father or face a new charge of treason. Ferdinand raged and sulked, but would not quit his throne.

His father and mother were spirited out of Spain (along with Godoy) in order to assist in the process of persuasion, but when the family was reunited everyone immediately started screaming at one another. Napoleon, disgusted by this unregal spectacle, ordered Ferdinand from the room. Ultimately, Ferdinand signed the abdication papers, and his father renounced his claim to the throne in favor of the French. Napoleon thereupon let it be known to a regency council organized by Murat in Madrid that his brother, Joseph, might be available if the Spanish people really wanted him. While the Bourbons were escorted to separate exiles in France, a deputation from Murat's puppet council appeared in Bayonne to offer the kingdom to Joseph.

There were those in Spain—Goya among them—who saw Joseph Bonaparte as a deliverer. He was a romantic and weak-willed man, but a paragon of virtue compared with the departed Bourbons and their crowd. He had proved himself a serious, adept and liberal-minded administrator in his previous post as Napoleon's appointed King of Naples, and he entered Madrid with the best of intentions, bringing with him from Bayonne a new constitution promising freedom, social and religious reform and just about everything else that the Spanish Enlightenment had either achieved or had been working toward. However, by the time Joseph arrived in Madrid, most of the country was up in arms.

As so often happens, the immediate cause of the revolution was a minor incident transformed through inept handling into a major crisis. On May 2, 1808, an order came from Napoleon that the last of Charles' sons, the 13-year-old Prince Francisco de Paula, should be conducted to Bayonne, leaving no member of the Royal Family on Spanish soil. A large crowd, more anxious than angry, gathered in the Plaza de Oriente, in front of the Royal Palace. They did not know the details of recent events, but they seemed to sense that a betrayal of some sort had been secretly taking place and that the removal of the Prince was a climax to the sellout. Until now they had been given no single event on which to focus their concern, only a series of *faits accomplis* against which protest would have been futile. Now, however, word reached them that the young Prince was tearfully resisting deportation—probably less from political principle than from a need to exercise the royal prerogative of throwing a temper tantrum. At last, though, the mob had a cause, and it threw itself upon the French soldiers who were to escort the Prince to exile. The soldiers responded with musketry. Unfortunately, the sound of battle brought the rest of the populace into the streets and, armed with improvised weapons, they fell upon Frenchmen wherever they found them. By evening, however, Murat had moved troops from the surrounding country into the city and, shooting and stabbing with disciplined ferocity, they broke up the mob. Firing squads worked through the night and into the morning hours, indiscriminately dispatching the mob's leaders and followers and, naturally, a large number of innocents. Within days, news of the revolt and its brutal suppression had spread through Spain; within months, resistance had been organized in every city and province. Indeed, by the middle of July, Spanish irregulars had forced a large body of French troops to surrender to them after a short siege at Bailén, and

Ferdinand VII symbolized Spanish revolt against the French in illustrations like the engraving above from an inflammatory broadside. Ferdinand points his sword toward the all-seeing eye of Providence, while the Spanish lion devours the Napoleonic eagle. Inscribed with patriotic doggerel, these leaflets urged the populace to rally to the banner of liberty that the cowardly Ferdinand never raised.

that defeat, in turn, forced the suddenly panicked French to abandon Madrid briefly. Spain had entered upon agony, an agony not to be ended until Napoleon was thoroughly defeated on other fields.

Two wars were fought in the Iberian Peninsula. One was a conventional war, waged between conventional armies, which marched and countermarched according to the rules of the game. In this war, history has named as the victor the Duke of Wellington, last and most successful commander of the expeditionary force Britain put ashore in Portugal in 1808. Like most such statements it is an oversimplification. It is true that Wellington entered Madrid in August 1812 and led his army to final victory at Vitoria in June 1813. On the other hand, some of the most important English triumphs were won by other generals, and some of their successes were simply handed them by Napoleon who had not assigned his best forces to the Spanish campaign, in the first place, and who, more significantly, was forced to withdraw troops from his Spanish second front in order to balance losses in Russia and elsewhere. Of at least as much significance to both Wellington and Napoleon—though neither ever admitted it—was the irregular warfare conducted by the Spanish people themselves. That war contributed a new word to the military lexicon—*guerrilla,* the name the Spanish themselves applied to the nonuniformed, ill-equipped spies, saboteurs and amateur soldiers who endlessly and savagely harrassed the invaders behind the lines.

The guerrilla effort was typically Spanish in that it was never properly organized or centrally controlled. Each of the impromptu governments, revolutionary juntas that sprang up after the May 2 revolt in Madrid, simply proceeded in its own way to take whatever toll it could from the invaders. All the arts of underground resistance with which the modern world is by now so familiar were practiced by them. The ambushed patrol, the bomb in the café, the poisoned water supply, the murdered courier—these were the routine events of guerrilla warfare, the second war. The French response to them has become equally familiar—the paranoid suspicion of the entire population, the brutal interrogation of prisoners; the exemplary, wholesale reprisals meted out to innocent and guilty alike; rape, looting and destruction at a level far higher than strict military necessity demanded. And, of course, there grew up a contempt for the adversary that prohibited the professional soldier from believing the evidence of his own eyes and prevented him from entertaining even the possibility that this rabble in arms might actually be defeating him in a slow, murderous, undramatic war of attrition.

Napoleon had, as a young man, exalted the memory of his Corsican forebears who had fought for their freedom in much the same manner as the Spanish were now doing. But he had come so far, so quickly from his background that he could not and would not see the analogy. "The Spanish people is vile and cowardly," he wrote, "about the same as I found the Arabs to be." Far from finding anything heroic in the Spanish resistance, Napoleon found it evidence of laziness and, by implication, of a lack of fitness for self-government in the modern world.

Thus the tragedy of Spain in the Napoleonic era: through its own lack of compassion, its blind insistence on rigorously imposing a conqueror's

Goya's portrait of Ferdinand VII was painted shortly after the ignoble monarch's return to the Spanish throne. The artist lavished meticulous attention on Ferdinand's glittering orders and ermine-lined cloak, while subtly revealing something of the personality of this arrogantly self-satisfied, despicable man, who has been called the worst king ever to sit on the Spanish throne.

will on a people that might have been won over by softer methods, France, a force for modernization more effective than any previously applied in Spain (a force, moreover, that began with sizable support among Spaniards), converted itself into the most hated oppressor in Spanish history. "I admit that I started off on the wrong foot in this whole business," Napoleon finally said. "The whole thing remains ugly. . . . And yet posterity would have commended my deed if I had succeeded."

Perhaps the most unfortunate of all the results of the French invasion was the conversion of the cowardly and stupid Ferdinand from a nonentity into "The Desired One," a hero whose return to power was the one war aim on which the entire nation agreed. Ironically, it was Ferdinand's restoration to the head of a repressive regime at the end of the war that effectively prevented Spain's participation in the great intellectual and industrial revolution of the 19th Century.

Still, the second of May, and the events that followed it, created, in a way that more peaceful efforts never had, a genuine national spirit in Spain. *Dos de Mayo* is Spain's Bastille Day, its Fourth of July, although its significance was not immediately apparent to most Spaniards.

Certainly it was not clear to Francisco Goya. He may have witnessed some of the events of that day, may even have made a few sketches for future reference. But his response to *Dos de Mayo,* like the rest of his behavior during the war years was, to say the least, ambiguous. Ultimately he would draw from this period the raw stuff for works that must be regarded among his greatest, but while the war proceeded he seemed to experience considerable difficulty in deciding which side he was on. Of course, he had to consider not only his personal survival but the conservation of the wealth he had accumulated through a lifetime's efforts. This was no small amount. When his wife died in 1812 an inventory showed that Goya possessed a home valued at 120,000 reales, with furniture worth about one tenth of that. His jewelry and silverware were estimated at some 52,000 reales, and he had cash in hand totaling close to 160,000 reales. All this was exclusive of paintings and prints by himself and others—considerably undervalued at around 12,000 reales—commissions for new works in hand, his ongoing salary from the court (which Joseph Bonaparte continued), the equipment in his studio and the house and securities he had already conveyed to his son. In short, the artist whom biographers have been pleased to portray as a romantic revolutionary presented, at this most revolutionary moment in his country's history, the aspect of a very comfortable bourgeois gentleman.

By and large, he acted the part. It is true that when it came time to oversee the hanging of his portrait of Ferdinand VII in the Royal Academy of San Fernando, he begged off in order to accept an invitation to go to Saragossa where, through the summer of 1808, guerrillas had conducted a heroic defense of the city. Goya wrote that he must go, "since the glory of my country is of such interest to me." So far as Goya knew, his patriotism was matched by his King's. He could not have known as he set out for Saragossa that its defenders were fighting in vain for a sovereign who was even then attempting to woo Napoleon's favor.

The visit to Saragossa was, however, Goya's last public acknowledg-

Canon Juan Antonio Llorente was a liberal clergyman, who, working from secret files, compiled the first factual history of the Inquisition, a body he had once served as secretary. In his portrait, Goya bared his sitter's dual nature—as a churchman and as a social reformer who welcomed the French —in the canon's fine, intelligent eyes and brow, his wily, almost sly, smile and his evident pride in wearing Joseph Bonaparte's decoration, the Royal Order of Spain.

ment of patriotic feelings. He was too old and too rich to give public allegiance to the resistance, and, as we shall see, he had reason to hope for some good from the French occupation. Thus, early in 1810, Goya was at work on a commission for the Madrid City Hall, an allegory in which Madrid is represented as a female figure, gesturing toward a medallion supported by winged spirits representing fame. In that medallion, originally, was a portrait of Joseph Bonaparte. Later, when Bonaparte lost the throne, his portrait was removed and the word "Constitución" was substituted, a tribute to a liberal document drawn up just prior to Ferdinand's restoration. When Ferdinand abrogated the constitution his portrait was substituted for the word. After his death he was painted out of the allegory just as his predecessor had been. Finally, the words *Dos de Mayo* were placed in the medallion—they remain there today. This oft-revised painting (Goya himself probably did not do the retouching) was by no means Goya's only involvement with the Napoleonic regime. He accepted a medal, the Order of Spain, from Joseph Bonaparte, a decoration that the people contemptuously called "the eggplant"; he attended the meeting of the Academy when it formally welcomed its new "protector," the Marquis of Almenara, an appointee of Joseph's. More important, Goya served on a committee charged with selecting 50 Spanish paintings that were to be shipped to Paris for inclusion in the Napoleon Museum, designed as a showcase for fine examples of the booty the Emperor collected on his campaigns. To his credit, Goya and his fellow committeemen were careful to choose the least important paintings they could find. Furthermore, they delayed the process of selection long enough for the tide of war to turn; the pictures never left Spain.

In addition, Goya painted portraits of such French officers as desired them, as well as a large number of their Spanish sympathizers—*afrancesados* as they were called. He had some justification for this use of his talent since this group formed the only market for the portraitist's art in those difficult days. Moreover, most of Goya's intellectual friends were, at least in the beginning, disposed to welcome the French as liberal-minded liberators, allies in a cause for which they had themselves long labored. Finally, some of Joseph Bonaparte's first projects were extremely appealing to Goya. He particularly appreciated the new King's order abolishing the Inquisition; one of Goya's finest portraits is of Juan Antonio Llorente, sometime secretary of the Inquisition's Madrid tribunal, who had opposed its operations so vehemently that he was finally dismissed from his post. The artist complemented this work with a series of pen-and-ink drawings, possibly intended for wider distribution as engravings, which savagely depicted the bad old days of the Inquisition at the height of its powers. Another Napoleonic edict, which shut down two thirds of Spain's religious houses, drew forth a similar series of sketches from the artist. These show some of the 60- or 70,000 monks and nuns, who were released from their vows, flinging off their clerical garb and, like children suddenly released from a strict school, throwing themselves into the pursuit of the worldly gratifications that were now available to them. These, too, never reached the engraver's plate.

Undoubtedly there was a certain amount of self-protectiveness in

Goya's attitude toward the French. But it is also clear that no reasonably dispassionate observer could believe their presence was a totally bad thing. To all but the most devoted adherents of the Bourbons, the meaning of the French presence in Spain was difficult to read, for, particularly at the outset, it offered in equal measure signs of hope and signals of fear.

The factor that turned Goya from a passively cooperative, possibly optimistic citizen of the new regime into a secret opponent—if not of its basic ideas then of its practical effects—was the length and bloodiness of the guerrilla war. By 1812 he had painted, evidently for his own eyes only, an oil entitled *The Colossus (page 129),* which, it has been appropriately suggested, might better be called "Panic." It shows a huge, nude male figure, tall enough to reach the sky, towering over a terrified crowd that streams away in all directions. It is an oppressive vision, painted with passion and cunning—some of the colors smeared on with a palette knife, others applied with a delicate split reed (a technique with which Goya was beginning to experiment). Its precise meaning is elusive. Is *The Colossus* intended to represent Napoleon and his effect on the Spanish people, or is he a more generalized symbol, perhaps of the god of war or the psychological terrors of social upheaval? And what of the crowd? Is Goya satirizing their panic, or is he perhaps commending it, since he shows only one figure, a donkey—his conventional symbol of stupidity—standing fast? What is very clear is that after four years of war, Goya was thoroughly sick of it, appalled by its terrible destructiveness and by the spiritual malaise that it was creating. The war was, for Goya, no longer a political issue; it was a moral one. No cause was worth so much bloodshed, no political principle worth so much agony—again, his revulsion is something a citizen of today can readily appreciate.

And so he began work on the red crayon drawings that would form the basis for his most powerful series of etchings, *The Disasters of War (pages 137-143).* There is nothing enigmatic about them, although scattered through the *Disasters* are allegorical compositions that suggest the monstrousness of conflict and its effect on the human spirit. (A "carnivorous vulture" perhaps signifies war, or parodies the eagle that was a symbol of Napoleonic rule. War may also be seen in a pig devouring its offspring.) But, as with the *Caprichos,* he found himself unable to follow his plans closely and the power of the *Disasters* lies not in generalizations but in terrible specificity. There is no doubt that Goya drew on his own observations—some of which were undoubtedly gathered in the course of his trip to Saragossa—as well as on the observations and anecdotes related to him by friends. Rape, torture, mass murder, the mutilation of corpses—etching after etching is devoted to these subjects, and in all of them victim and victimizer alike are reduced to a state less than human. Goya's infinitely subtle style achieves the frightful, exaggerated clarity of a dream vision, yet never loses touch with waking reality and never quite descends to the sort of fantastical caricature that marked the *Caprichos.* There is no vagueness, no mystery here, but rather a heightened realism transcending the usual limits of the realistic esthetic to give us a glimpse not of the imagined underworld but of hell on earth, hell man-made.

Goya worked at a more deliberate pace on these etchings than he did on the *Caprichos*. He is known to have begun the series during the war, for two of the drawings and three prints are dated 1810, but he may not have finished work on the plates until the war had been over for several years. This lack of urgency indicates that his purpose was not primarily propagandistic. Indeed, given his circumspect nature, it is doubtful that he dared entertain the notion of publishing such visions during such unsettled times. In fact, it is no easier to read the true political intentions of the *Disasters* than it is to read Goya's true thoughts about the war. His apologists have made much of the fact that he was careful to show the soldiery wearing French uniforms, but he was also careful to show Spanish partisans engaged in activity no less reprehensible than that of the foreign troops. A traditional story recounts Goya's servant asking him, "Why do you paint these barbarities that men commit?" and Goya replying, "To tell men forever that they should not be barbarians."

Even after the war Goya made no effort to publish the *Disasters*, knowing they could only offend the restored King and his court by reminding them of their responsibility for the *desastres de la guerra*. Though Goya gave his friend Ceán Bermúdez an album containing a proof set of the series so that he might correct the epigraphs and the title page, the entire set remained unpublished until 1863—35 years after Goya's death —when the Academy of San Fernando brought out a complete edition.

O ne gathers that *The Disasters of War* was a subject that imposed itself upon Goya, a subject he would gladly have avoided if his imagination had let him. The uncharacteristic slowness with which he worked on the series, the care with which both in the etchings and in his public career he refused to commit himself definitively to either side in the war, his eagerness whenever possible to turn to morally neutral subjects—all this argues that Goya did not find in the war a psychologically liberating subject comparable to the *Caprichos*. Rather, it was irresistible, something so perfectly suited to his talent as to be unavoidable.

The fact remains, however, that in the midst of war's terrors and agitations Goya somehow managed to devote at least as much energy to material that was escapist, merely delightful. During the war years he turned out a lovely series of intimate portraits: placid, limpid, wonderfully gentle and sympathetic. Among his subjects were his son's mother-in-law and father-in-law; his grandson Mariano, who was the delight of his later years; three other children of prominent Madrileños; the actress Antonia Zárate; the strikingly beautiful Francisca Sabasa García.

When he was not executing these portraits, he turned to ordinary life and labor for subject matter in such paintings as *The Water Carrier, The Knife Sharpener* and, greatest of all, *The Forge*, a masterful study in human strength and energy applied to the work of a blacksmith shop. Nor did he ignore his beloved *majas,* painting several versions of the *Majas on a Balcony (page 25)* in which the beautiful girls lean coquettishly forward while their *majos,* swathed in sinister cloaks and almost hidden under their bicorn hats, glower in the background. He painted women of the same class in *The Love Letter* and, reverting to themes from the *Caprichos,* he painted *Old Age*—a comical satire—and *Celestina and Her Daughter*—statements of his fascination with the contrast between the

In this portrait of General Juan Martin, Goya depicted the fierce peasant pride and bravado that earned the guerrilla leader his nickname of *El Empecinado* (The Indomitable). Martin was ill paid for his years of harrying the French invaders; on Ferdinand's return to Madrid the peasant hero was jailed, and although he escaped, he was recaptured, tortured and ignominiously put to death.

beauty of youth and the inescapable tragedy of its destruction by the passage of time. In a sense, all of these pictures are final statements on subjects that had long preyed upon him. Now, however, Goya draws back from his subjects, allowing them to speak for themselves. He now has the confidence of old age and professionalism in the rightness of his eye, his heart, his mind. He feels serene in the belief that what he wishes to paint is intrinsically interesting and without need of artificial emotional color or flavor.

The contrast between the expressive mode of these pictures and the *Disasters* could not be more striking. One imagines Goya resenting the necessity of doing the latter, and can almost hear him crying out for surcease from the emotions the war created in him and that he was compelled to discharge in those etchings. It is the paintings, not the work on the copper plates, that seem most expressive of his deepest mood, his fondest wish for an enterprise to occupy his old age.

Even his portrayals of Madrid's last conqueror, the Duke of Wellington, suggest this mood. He met Wellington on the night the Duke entered the capital, and the pencil sketch he made at that time reflects not triumph but a weariness that the painter profoundly understood. The half-length portrait *(page 136)*, that Goya later produced is similarly lacking in heroism—it is not more than a good likeness and is perhaps evidence of a fundamental lack of emotional contact between sitter and painter. Finally, in an equestrian portrait, the "Iron Duke" is seen almost wryly by the artist, "a casual conqueror," as Michael Levey puts it, "an eccentric private gentleman rather than a victorious general."

Nevertheless, Wellington's victorious campaign, coupled with the birth of a viable nationalism, a product of the resistance, gave Goya and the rest of the liberal community reason to hope that some good might come of the war. A liberal-minded Cortes (Parliament) had functioned as a kind of government in exile in besieged Cádiz throughout most of the war, and in 1812 it had drafted a constitution guaranteeing a degree of political and religious freedom. Though incomplete, these freedoms were greater than any previously written into law. Early in 1814 the Cortes established a regency council in Madrid until the government could be turned over to Ferdinand, whom it hoped would swear allegiance to the new constitution and become a monarch of limited power.

It was to a member of this regency council, Cardinal Don Luis de Bourbon (Goya had painted him as a child long ago at the court of his father, the Infante), that the artist wrote expressing his ardent desire "to perpetuate with the brush the most notable and heroic deeds or scenes of our glorious insurrection against the tyrant of Europe." Ever the shrewd guardian of his career, the painter was at last ready to make a public comment—the *Disasters* were unpublished as yet—and the council accepted the offer, though not with any notable enthusiasm.

The romantic tale, first related by an imaginative servant, which had Goya prowling the streets of Madrid on the night of *Dos de Mayo* in order to sketch by lantern light the horrible consequences of that outburst of revolutionary fervor, has no basis in truth. But it does appear that Goya, like all residents of the capital, had some direct knowledge of the day's events and that during the war years he made sketches and color notes for some commemorative paintings. Now was the time to finish these paintings and present them to the government.

They are, of course, among the most famous of Goya's works—*The Second of May 1808, in Madrid (pages 130-131)*, commemorating the uprising against the Mamelukes of the Napoleonic Cavalry, and *The Third of May 1808, in Madrid (pages 132-135)*, documenting the shooting of the Spaniards by the French. They are huge canvases—roughly 9 feet high and 12 feet across—and they are painted with a passion that, even for Goya, is remarkable. They have been subjected to criticism through the years the charge of the Mamelukes (Arab mercenaries recruited by Napoleon in Egypt) has no compositional center, is a confused jumble, is suffused in an odd, greenish light; the firing squad scene is oddly cramped, all wrong as to perspective, since Goya had to cram into it both victims and executioners. And yet, despite their flaws, despite the mixture of motives that impelled Goya to his task, they are great paintings. The Impressionists of 19th Century France correctly saw in them the beginnings of their style (Manet was to recall the composition of Goya's firing squad picture when he painted *The Execution of the Emperor Maximilian)*; it is precisely because Goya did not attempt to give his viewers the pleasure of formal correctness that the pictures are so powerful—an anarchical technique reflects and vivifies war's anarchy. Goya's portrayal of the executioners of May 3 as anonymous (their heads are hidden as they aim their rifles), and the terror he reveals in their victim— his comrades cowering or already sprawled in awkward death, his arms upraised, eyes glued in terror on the guns—is an unforgettable confrontation between naked power and the defenseless individual.

By the time Goya finished the pictures, however, both the regency council and the constitutional Cortes had been abandoned. Immediately on returning to Spanish soil, Ferdinand broke contact with the liberals. Supported by the so-called *serviles* (the Church and the large landowners), he established an absolutist government based on the prewar model.

The Crown nevertheless accepted Goya's pictures, conveniently forgetting its role in bringing the French to Spain in the first place and enjoying its image as a victim of tyranny no less heroic than the people. At first the new regime was not outwardly harsh, and Goya discovered that he could get along with it about as well as he had with that of Ferdinand's late father (Charles IV had died in exile in 1819). He discharged one last debt to Spanish patriotism by painting a heroic portrait of General Palafox, defender of Saragossa, and then demonstrated fealty to the new ruler by making no less than four portraits of him, all based on a single study, though none were commissioned by the Crown itself. Thereafter, as the habits of peace were resumed, commissions for new portraits again poured in, among them orders for studies of a whole new generation of Osunas. In the period between his 66th and 68th birthdays, Goya had reason to hope that the outward mood of his world would be reflected in a new inner tranquility, that anxiety, the great constant of his life until then, would finally depart and allow him to enjoy the fruits of his labors and his years in peace.

Homage to the Bulls

Since the dim days of prehistory, the men of the Iberian Peninsula have fought the bulls that roam their vast plains. Wild beasts were distinctively drawn on the cave walls by the early men who hunted them, as may be seen at Altamira in northern Spain. Throughout the centuries mounted riders—warriors, nobles and even kings—tested their courage against the brave bulls. Today, professional *toreros* continue this tradition by challenging bulls especially bred to fight. Until more recent times, this national passion regularly met official resistance: various monarchs outlawed it; those who participated were threatened with excommunication by papal decree. But the Spaniards stubbornly clung to the bullfight—the ceremony of a powerful animal being dominated, then dispatched, by a skilled man. In time, the contest developed into the solemn, and highly ritualized, pageant of the *fiesta de toros.*

As befit a robust, fiery Spaniard of provincial background, Goya was fascinated by the bulls. Some romantic biographers even claim he was once a professional *torero.* There is no proof of this, but only an artist thoroughly familiar with bulls could impart the vitality, accuracy and astonishing psychological realism to the bullfight that Goya does. This is particularly true in his later work, his lithographs, paintings and his inspired *Tauromaquia,* a series of etchings originally intended as illustrations for a history of bullfighting.

Among Goya's first illustrations in the *Tauromaquia* is one showing how, in ages past, wild bulls were fought by riders wielding lances, aided by footmen who tied the bull's legs with rope *(above, right).* In time bullfights became so popular that Spaniards liked to believe that their greatest national hero, the 11th Century warrior El Cid, fought them. Goya tried to substantiate this myth when he drew El Cid in action *(below, right).* But his drawing contains a glaring anachronism; the costume El Cid wears is of the period of Charles I, who really did fight bulls in tournaments, but who lived almost 500 years later.

Modo con que los antiguos españoles cazaban   The way in which the ancient Spaniards hunted
los toros á caballo en el campo   the bulls on horseback in the open country

El Cid Campeador lanceando otro toro   The Cid Campeador spearing another bull

Ligereza y atrevimiento de Juanito Apiñani en la plaza de Madrid   The ability and audacity of Juanito Apiñani in the ring at Madrid

Bullfighting, which began as an informal sport waged in the fields between horsemen armed with lances and wild bulls, changed in the 16th Century to a formal confrontation in the tournaments of the ruling lords, taking its place beside such traditional chivalric contests as jousting. In this way it was established as an accepted method for the nobles to prove their bravery. This aristocratic phase of fighting bulls on horseback ended after about 600 years of practice when Philip V, the first of the French Bourbon monarchs, forbade his nobles to risk their lives in this way. Instead of withering away after the aristocracy dropped it, bullfighting was taken up eagerly by the masses, as brave young men of the lower classes began to fight the bulls on foot.

Goya traces some of this history in the *Tauromaquia*, but very early in the series he wanders from the glories of the past and turns to what he has seen and heard about. He shows acrobatic young *toreros*, like Juanito Apiñani, electrifying crowds by vaulting over a charging bull *(above)*, baiting them while standing on tables and killing them with swords while seated on chairs. Such bravura is rare in bullfights today, but the framework for modern fights was being slowly built; *toreros* moved around the ring on foot using a large Spanish cape to deceive the bull into making passes that swept the horns close to the man's body. The development of the muleta, a fan-shaped cape that concealed the sword, gave the *torero* a new freedom to step forward and kill the bull face to face instead of dispatching it with a lance from horseback.

The inventor of the muleta was Francisco Romero, who came from Ronda, a little mountain town not far from Granada where Spain's first bull ring was built in 1775. Francisco was the patriarch of a major dynasty of *toreros* that included his grandson, Pedro *(opposite, above)*, who by his own account killed about 5,600 bulls in 28 years of fighting. Perhaps the most popular *torero* in Goya's day, however, was Pepe Illo who, after surviving 13 serious gorings during 30 years of fighting, died under the horns of a bull on May 11, 1801 *(opposite, below)*. His death became a legend overnight. But Pepe Illo was more than a folk hero; the year before he died he wrote the first definitive account of modern bullfighting, a work that laid down the rules for the *toreros*, who fought on foot—rules that in time evolved into the ritual of today's fight.

Pedro Romero matando á toro parado   Pedro Romero killing the halted bull

La desgraciada muerte de Pepe Illo en la plaza de Madrid   The unlucky death of Pepe Illo in the ring at Madrid

El famoso Americano, Mariano Ceballos   The famous American, Mariano Ceballos

Dibersion de España   Spanish Entertainment

Bullfight in a Village, 1808-1809

The bullfights Goya saw offered a variety of arresting sights. Some of the scenes are familiar today, like the mounted picador *(above)* about to bury his pike into the neck muscle of the bull and thus literally bleed some of the energy from the beast. Other scenes were more bizarre and seemed to linger, like odd dreams, in Goya's mind for his entire life. After he had completed the *Tauromaquia* and was an old man living in Bordeaux, he discovered lithography and immediately employed it to memorialize his beloved bull ring. In one lithograph, Mariano Ceballos, a South American Indian who was a *torero* in

Spain during the late 18th Century, rides one bull while attacking another *(opposite, above)*. In *Spanish Entertainment (opposite, below)*, the crowd at a fight spills from the stands to form a human circle around the bulls and taunt them. One man tries to lure the bull into a pass with a piece of his clothing even while the animal is goring another man on the ground. The seething mob, the slightly grotesque faces, the air of complete abandon, all exuberantly discharge the spirit of intoxication, both literal and figurative, of the Spanish peasants taking part in an 18th Century bullfight.

161

To those who have seen or read about a modern bullfight, some of Goya's work, like *The Bullfight (right)*, must seem strange. The mass confusion of the crowd inside the ring is a far cry from the 20th Century *corrida*, which is a succession of dignified rituals—the elegant swirl of a *torero's* cape as a fresh, brave bull rushes by; the proud air of the man stalking his prey with a muleta; the *torero's* exultant tour of the ring after a particularly skillful kill to receive flowers dropped by demure ladies or to squeeze wine from skins tossed by admiring men. In the modern fight, the *torero* stands with his entourage to face the bull while the crowd remains in the stands.

But in Goya's time, the crowd did not merely sit back to enjoy the fight vicariously; it joined in. Men and boys streamed into the ring to run, taunt and swarm around the bulls. In this painting, Goya strikingly conveys the sense of tumult by the use of streaks and blobs of paint placed on the canvas with split reeds or palette knives. His free-and-easy style marvelously recreates the near-chaos in the ring.

The Bullfight, c. 1827

VIII

The
Serene
Exile

The brilliant insights and tough
determination that helped make
Goya one of the greatest of all
portraitists are evident in this self-
portrait done when he was in his
early seventies. Abjuring any
details that might divert the
viewer, Goya finds in himself a
deaf, slightly tired old man, whose
face still transmits the vitality that
would endure for the last 10 years
of his life.

Self-Portrait, 1815

Peace was to be temporary and illusory in Spain. The country was bank-
rupt, and Ferdinand was forced to float an endless series of small loans
merely to maintain the royal residences and pay his servants. The royal
household was not difficult to manage, but the huge army left standing
by the war was. A portion of it could be employed in the frustrating, ultimately fruitless task of reasserting Spain's influence in its South
American colonies, nearly all of which were now in revolt, but even the
soldiers thus employed were often unpaid and, on occasion, unfed. Others idled in cantonments in Spain or were mustered out into a depressed
economy that, aside from a woefully inadequate number of government
jobs, offered them no employment. In a few years this army would form
the cadre for a revolution that would briefly impose upon Ferdinand the
liberal constitution that the Cortes had been unable to make him accept.
During the period 1814-1820, however, the army, sullen but quiescent,
was both a symbol and a cause of the nation's unrest.

For Goya, the discomforts and disappointments of the post-war period were particularly difficult to bear. Despite his years and infirmities,
he still had a tremendous amount of creative energy that he found difficult to discharge. After 1815 there were few works for him to do at
court. He painted only an occasional portrait, and he no longer mingled
much in society. Many of his best and oldest friends were dead, some
had gone into exile in France, still others had withdrawn from active participation in public affairs. Never the best tempered of men, Goya
appears to have grown less able than ever to suffer fools. Even his relations with his son were once again strained and distant though they
never disintegrated into a complete and open break. Goya now stayed
close to his studio, where his principal preoccupation was his *Tauromaquia,* a set of 44 etchings (only 33 were published), originally conceived
as illustrations for the *Historical Note Concerning the Origin and Development of Bullfighting in Spain,* written by his friend, Nicolás Fernández de
Moratín, in 1777. As before, however, Goya found it impossible to
maintain his original intention when he began work on the plates *(pages
157-159).* Approximately at mid-point, he abandoned history and began

to speak personally about the bulls. He drew upon his own memories of great moments in the ring, rather than upon Moratín's text, and apotheosized such matadors of his time as Martincho, Pedro Romero and Pepe Illo, heroes of an era when the traditions of the bull ring were being developed. In the realistic *Tauromaquia* prints, as in the greatest *corridas* themselves, puny man meets an animal representing the force of the irrational—a basic confrontation around which so much of Spanish culture, so much of Goya's own work, revolves. The symbols here are obvious, unstrained, and the etchings are wonderfully dynamic works charged by the artist's passion for his subject. The *Tauromaquia* also has another dimension, a dimension of delight, for it is clearly the work of an artist indulging himself, relaxing with his memories of a spectacle that had been his favorite form of recreation and release since childhood.

Release. That was what Goya craved in these years—release from concern with the world of political and social intrigue, release from the demands of patrons and the importunings of acquaintances. Release, in short, from responsibility for a public self and career. The *Tauromaquia* was a project in this new mood and so, too, was another great self-portrait *(page 164)*, executed sometime after his 70th birthday. He is heavier now, and his eyes no longer flash as they did in previous portrayals. Instead, they are weary and rather guarded. Still, the thinning hair has grayed only at the temples, and there is a firmness in the set of mouth and chin that indicates neither self-pity nor fear. Goya is, at least, a man who seems to know himself and the world and to accept the reality of both. It is the least complicated of his self-portraits. Like all of his art of this time, it had been simplified in composition and technique.

Subject matter was no longer a prime concern with Goya. What increasingly interested him was the process of painting itself. The rules of composition, the necessity for getting "a good likeness," the need to make meanings clear to anyone other than himself no longer interested him. What now obsessed him was what might be called technique under pressure; his work became a series of experiments with the application of paint to canvas, with impressionistic rather than realistic colors, with radical simplification of composition and, indeed, of human features. Clearly, the *Caprichos* had made Goya realize that he could get powerful effects by working merely in monochrome and by deviating from the realistic. This realization inspired him to further efforts in the same direction. In previous works he had attempted to gain a new texture by using a split reed as a brush; in all the paintings of the war and post-war period he tried similar experiments to gain more power, more emotion. The paint is daubed on, scraped, scratched, worked and modeled.

His interest in new methods extended beyond painting to graphics, and so it was characteristic of him that, at age 73, he became the first major artist to try the new process of lithography, which had been invented in Bavaria in 1796. Lithography was vastly less time consuming than the etching techniques Goya had previously employed, easily permitting the artist to transfer an ink or crayon drawing to the printing surface or, indeed, to draw directly upon the limestone block that is the printing plate. Eliminated is the laborious task of scratching the original

This engraving, one of the very few known pictures of the Quinta del Sordo, shows Goya's retreat on the outskirts of Madrid near the Manzanares River many years after he bought the estate in 1819. After Goya had remodeled the modest house, each of its two stories contained a 30-by-18-foot chamber flanked by smaller rooms. A stream, which was a delight in arid Spain, rippled through the tree-set grounds and probably fed the marble fountain shown here.

composition into the printing plate and then etching the plate in acid.

Lithography suited Goya's impatient work method, granted him access to striking new effects—great freedom of line and rich, dense blacks are possible in lithography. This willingness to experiment was the most engaging quality about Goya's later years. He simply would not settle himself in a rut. In 1819, the same year that he tried his hand at lithography, he finally decided that he had had enough of Madrid, and he bought a country estate—"twenty-two acres of sowing land, with a house . . . beyond the Segovia Bridge . . . on the site where the Hermitage of the Holy Guardian Angel formerly stood," according to the deed. The house, for which he paid 60,000 reales in cash, was "of brick and adobe, with a garden attached, two floors divided into several rooms, a well of drinking water immediately adjoining the said garden and another in the courtyard, and two attics; furthermore, by the stream, in the center . . . five white poplars." By a curious coincidence, the house next door was known locally as the Quinta del Sordo (the House of the Deaf Man) because its owner also suffered Goya's affliction. After Goya's death, his own house became the famous Quinta del Sordo.

Goya immediately set about enlarging and improving his real estate—adding wells, ponds, springs, fences and even a vineyard. His intention was not to create a showplace, only a comfortable retreat. But perhaps he was encouraged to go a little farther in this effort than he might otherwise have done because he seems to have been accompanied in his self-imposed exile by a handsome and extraordinarily enigmatic lady named Leocadia Weiss and her daughter, five-year-old Rosarito. It is generally believed that Doña Leocadia was a distant relative of the painter, but, in fact, little is known about her before she appeared in Goya's life. She had been married to one Isidoro Weiss, the merchant son of a German who had emigrated to Spain. Their separation has been attributed to her tongue, which was reputed by gossip to be one of the most shrewish in Madrid. But this, of course, would have made no impact on the deaf Goya, who had apparently taken up with her shortly after his wife died. It is also widely supposed that little Rosarito was his daughter. Certainly he loved her as if she were his own.

The child and her mother—who acted as housekeeper and probably as mistress—were to stay with Goya until the end of his life. To all appearances, he was completely happy with this arrangement, particularly after 1819 when he suffered another serious illness. Doña Leocadia nursed him, the child brightened his sickroom and Goya recovered strength enough to resume painting early in 1820. Just how seriously he took this illness is evidenced by two things: he painted more than one copy of a picture showing his doctor, Eugenio García Arrieta, treating him. And, when he returned to work, he immediately took up those instruments of his despairing moods, his engraver's tools.

Many explanations have been put forth for these last etchings. In all, 22 plates seem to belong to an unfinished series, four of which were left out of the first edition, which was brought out by the Academy of San Fernando in 1864. The Academy titled its edition *Los Proverbios,* but the prints are best known as the *Disparates (pages 116-119),* the plural of the

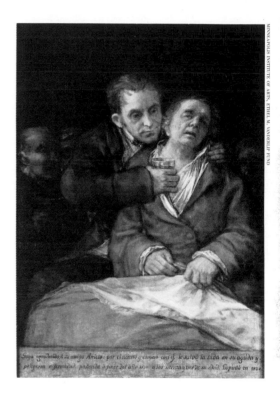

Soon after moving into his country house, Goya once again fell desperately ill. In gratitude to Eugenio García Arrieta, the distinguished physician who cured him, he painted this unusual and moving portrait of himself and his doctor. It is inscribed: "Goya thanks his friend Arrieta for the care and attention with which he saved his life in the acute and dangerous illness suffered at the end of the year 1819 at the age of 73. He painted this in 1820."

word Goya most frequently employed in his captions. It is a word for which there is no precise English equivalent, though "folly" or "absurdity" come closest to the Spanish *disparate*.

Goya's conscious intention in the *Disparates* was undoubtedly to catalogue the many stupidities and absurdities of life. Among them are the follies of frivolous woman, of marriage, of poverty, of war, of carnival, even that of his beloved bulls, shown gamboling through the air. Based loosely on familiar proverbs of the day, these plates, somewhat larger than Goya's previous etchings, have an even more fantastical air than the *Caprichos*. The dark backgrounds, dramatic effects of light and huge, distorted forms give the *Disparates* a unique dreamlike quality.

After he had sufficiently recovered his health, Goya launched himself on his last, vast undertaking, the famous "Black Paintings" *(pages 173-185)*. These huge murals in oil, comparable in the size of the figures to the frescoes in San Antonio de la Florida but intended for Goya's eyes only, were painted directly on the plaster walls of the two largest rooms in the Quinta del Sordo. They must be understood as recapitulations of the major themes of Goya's life and art.

They are, to begin with, remarkably original in conception. All artists, of course, live intensely with their work, but until Goya painted these pictures no one had tried to live *in* his work. Here he was not merely transferring the images of his unconscious to canvas or paper but also attempting to materialize the immaterial world of his mind in such a way that these images would form a total environment. Instead of body containing mind, Goya was trying to make the mind contain his body. This group of 14 paintings can be seen as a primitive, instinctual attempt at self-analysis, having the same end as modern psychoanalysis, in which the patient brings out and lives openly with his secret thoughts, harmlessly discharging a force that is potentially self-destructive when it is kept locked in the silent darkness of the mind.

In particular, Goya wanted to state the irreconcilable conflicts that he, Spain and the entire world always live with and always try to deny. It is therefore essential to consider the individual paintings not as disconnected entities but as intimately related parts of a whole, to try to visualize them as they were in their original context in Goya's home.

Flanking the main door in the largest downstairs room are a full-length portrait *(page 178)* of a strikingly beautiful woman (alleged to be Doña Leocadia) and an equally long, narrow study of two men, one very aged and calm, the other agitated and evil, whispering in his elder's ear. The woman seems to represent healthy, relatively youthful sensuality, and the men its opposite. Across the room the Biblical Judith *(page 179)* brandishes a knife, ready for her famous kill—yet another example of Goya's obsession with feminine violence. On the same wall, next to Judith, Saturn *(page 185)* crushes his son in his huge hands and lifts him to his bloody maw, a symbol of the incomprehensible irrationality of the universe and a statement of corrupt paternalism, as Judith may be a symbol of maternalism perverted. On the long walls of the room two giant, crowded canvases confront one another. One depicts *The Vision of the Pilgrims of San Isidro (pages 182-184)* and recalls Goya's sketch for the

Self-exiled and about 80 years old, Goya captioned this sketch of a bearded ancient indomitably hobbling from darkness toward the light, "Still I learn." The painter, whose steps had begun to falter, was indeed still learning; he had started painting miniatures on ivory, in a manner never tried before; and he had recently mastered the newly invented techniques of lithography. In no way a physical self-portrait, the drawing—one of Goya's last—nonetheless expresses his own unconquerable spirit.

unfinished tapestry cartoon about this festival. Here, however, darkness has settled completely over the scene, there is desperation in the gaiety that distorts the faces of the singers who dominate the picture and distraction in the huddled, shrouded figures who are seen as little more than shadows. Still, this is essentially an innocent crowd, a trifle frightened by the gloom, but hardly responsible for it. This cannot be said of the mob that confronts it across the room in the *Witches' Sabbath (pages 180-182)*. But this satanic scene is no longer seen in the cheerfully satirical light of the little witchcraft painting Goya did more than a quarter of a century earlier for the Duke and Duchess of Osuna *(page 84)*. Face after face in this crowd has taken on an animalistic expression; locked in superstition, each has lost its human qualities. They have, it seems, brought this loss on themselves by dabbling in the black arts, and Goya has painted into this scene both his unceasing hatred of irrationality and his continuing attraction to it. Along with the *San Isidro,* the painting is a brutal comment on man in the mass, on the dehumanization that results when an individual allows himself to be subsumed by the mob.

I n the room on the floor above this one, the study in contrasts proceeds. *Two Grinning Women* grimace horribly and *Two Old Men* shovel gruel into their toothless lips: the females' laughter seems almost to mingle in the air with the senile cacklings of the ancients. Next to the women, and in contrast to them and to all the "Black Paintings" except the picture of the young woman, is *The Reading,* an act of faith in reason amidst the madness of the world. The big pictures in this room are four —a brutal *Fight with Clubs (pages 173-174)*; *The Pilgrimage to the Miraculous Fountain of San Isidro,* in which the pilgrims are seen streaming away from the light (of reason?) and into a dark forest (of religion?); *The Fates,* hovering with unconcealed glee above the world, waiting to strike down one and all; a *Fantastic Vision (pages 175-177),* in which two figures levitate toward a city on a rock, floating above a crowd, but unaware of two soldiers who have raised their rifles to take aim.

There is one last picture in this room. At first glance it appears to be an abstraction in brown and gold tones, but then one perceives in it a sad dog—a very humble mongrel struggling feebly, but gamely, against the tides of earth, barely keeping his head up where he can breathe. One cannot help but think that this may be Goya's last self-portrait, a study not of his features, but of his spirit, fighting for life against the encroaching world, the encroaching disorder of his mind.

Perhaps this is true, for the "Black Paintings" finally seem to be an act of the most tremendous creative courage for this aging, often ailing, spiritually and physically isolated man, an act in which he turned around and confronted, with anger, honesty and even humor, all the furies that had so long pursued him and, by so doing, finally exorcised them. It is all here, everything that Goya knew, everything he really cared about—his love-hate relationships with women, the irrational, the superstitious, the religious; his love of man alone, and his hate of man in the mass; his loathing of old age, his sustaining faith in reason and in the lonely courage of the man who clings to it in an unreasonable world. In summing himself up one last time, he also summed up the enigma of Spain, the land riven by contrasts and conflicts, where all during Goya's life the forces of light and darkness contended for the souls and bodies of men and where neither side has, even now, claimed a final victory.

Goya could, however, claim a victory, though only a private one. (The "Black Paintings" did not become known until 50 years after his death, when they were removed from the walls of the house, transferred to canvas and exhibited at the Paris Exposition of 1878.) That he created in privacy did not seem to bother Goya. After a lifetime's lust for fame he seemed positively relieved not to have to bother about it anymore. In any case, the "Black Paintings" represent a last leaping up of the flames before a fire begins to burn low and starts to die. He still had a few major works left in him, but no more projects on a scale such as this.

Indeed, in the year after he completed the "Black Paintings" he was mostly preoccupied by the need to insure his own safety and that of his new dependents, Doña Leocadia and her daughter. In 1823 Ferdinand swept constitutional government aside once again and enforced his brand of absolutism on Spain, this time with a harshness that frightened Goya, who had openly supported a new, short-lived constitution. He went into hiding for a short time, deeding the country house over to his grandson, Mariano, who was now 17 years old, and going to live for three months in the home of Don José de Duaso y Latre, a friend who was editor of an influential newspaper and therefore able to offer Goya protection. Since he had not made a single official public appearance since 1820 and had had little to do with political life in Madrid prior to that, his fears were probably groundless, especially since Ferdinand now decided to pose as culture's friend. (In 1819 he had created the Prado Museum— the only act for which Spain owes him any thanks.) In May 1824, Goya felt secure enough to address the Palace directly, requesting a leave of absence for six months—he was still officially First Painter to the King— in order to take the waters at Plombières in France.

When he set forth from Spain, however, it was not for the famous resort. Instead, he stopped briefly in Bordeaux, where his friend, the poet and playwright Leandro Fernández de Moratín, son of the bullfight historian, was living in exile. Moratín found Goya "deaf, old, slow and weak, not knowing a word of French, and so happy and so desirous of seeing the world." Goya lingered there for only three days before pressing on to Paris. The old man even managed to do a little painting—a bullfight, portraits of two prominent Spaniards—and penned a self-portrait before returning to Bordeaux in September and settling down, first in a room, then in "a comfortable little house," which was new, had a garden and was quite isolated from its neighbors.

In Bordeaux he painted Moratín's portrait and that faithful friend left an excellent record of Goya's stay there. "Goya is here with his Doña Leocadia," he wrote, adding, "I do not observe in them the least harmony." The painter, however, remained unconcerned. "He likes the city, the countryside, the climate, the food, and the independence and tranquility which he can enjoy." He also delighted in the companionship of little Rosarito who, within a year, was speaking French "like a skylark" and making friends with schoolmates her own age. Together, she and

Goya made drawings and embarked on a little artistic adventure—painting miniatures, something he had never tried. Goya was ecstatic about the child's gift, boasting that she was "perhaps the greatest phenomenon of her age in the world, to do what she does."

Even another illness could not dampen the artist's spirits for long. He languished only a few months, and then Moratín was writing: "Goya has escaped Charon's avaricious clutches this time; he is very spirited and painting vigorously, without wanting ever to correct what he has painted." He also returned to the lithographer's stone, placing it on his easel as if it were canvas. He "managed his pencils like brushes, without sharpening them," a contemporary reported, " . . . standing, constantly stepping back and forward to judge the effect" and producing his last splendid graphics, known as *The Bulls of Bordeaux (page 160).*

He even found, in the following year, his 80th, the strength to make a farewell visit to Madrid, perhaps to see his son and grandson, but principally to renew his permission to stay abroad. While there, he allowed himself to be painted by Vicente López, who had succeeded Goya as the city's fashionable portraitist and First Painter to the King. He returned home to Bordeaux to more leisurely labors—some drawings, a masterful portrait of a friend, Juan de Muguiro, and a picture into which he poured all the sunshine of his exile years, the *Milkmaid of Bordeaux.*

In February 1828, Goya wrote asking his grandson Mariano and his wife to come to Bordeaux, and in late March they arrived. Mariano allowed Goya to append a few lines to a note he was sending to his father in Spain: "I can only say that I have become a little indisposed with so much happiness, and am in bed. God grant that I may see you come to seek them [his family], for that would make my pleasure complete."

Xavier, however, could not arrive in time. On April 2, his saint's day, Goya awoke at dawn, unable to speak, his side paralyzed. Speech returned, but not the ability to move. "Thus he was for 13 days," Doña Leocadia later wrote Moratín, who was away in Paris at the time. "He would look at his hand, but as if stupified; he wanted to make a will, he said, in our favor, and his daughter-in-law replied that he already had. After that he was not out of danger for a moment . . . weakness impeded the limited understanding of what he said, and he rambled . . . he died at about 2 in the morning on the night of the 15th-16th . . . so serenely, and departed as one asleep; even the doctor was astonished at his courage; he said he did not suffer at all, but I am not so sure of that!"

If he did suffer in death, it must have seemed as nothing to him compared to the sufferings he had witnessed and undergone in the course of his long, vexing, confused and erratic life. Indeed, the calm and brightness of his last four years indicates that Goya was quite ready for this final release, that he felt he had left nothing undone. He had painted his age and in so doing had captured forever "the black magic of our civilization" as the poet Baudelaire put it. In the process of finding the artistic freedom he needed for this great act of creation he had broken free of all the old restraints, discovering almost by accident the freedom from which all of modern art has taken its cue. There was nothing more—and nothing less—for him to have done.

Vicente López, Goya's successor as First Painter to the King, portrayed his 80-year-old predecessor at the command of King Ferdinand VII. Goya had left Bordeaux, where he was living in quiet isolation, to ask the anti-liberal King for permission to retire from court service. In Madrid Goya met with unexpected kindness; the King accepted his resignation graciously, ordered this portrait to be painted, granted Goya a pension and let the dauntless old artist return to France.

The "Black Paintings"

There were few visitors to La Quinta del Sordo (the House of the Deaf Man)—the handsome country retreat outside Madrid that Goya bought in 1819 when he was 72. The aged artist, already isolated by his deafness and recuperating from the second near-fatal illness of his long life, lived there in seclusion. After being at the center of Spanish life for years, his only companions were an earthy housekeeper and her young daughter, who may have been a child of Goya's.

Had guests ever toured the inside of this house, it is not likely they would ever have forgotten the haunting pictures Goya had painted on the walls. Upstairs there were eight, including the one at right. Downstairs there were six, equally strange and morbid. These arresting scenes, sometimes vividly colored but generally dark in their themes, were Goya's most personal and emotional statements, his "Black Paintings"—the creatures of his fertile imagination. They were not commissioned by any patron and were never intended to leave his retreat. And they would probably be there to this day had not an admiring art collector had them lifted off the walls, transferred to canvas and removed in 1874. Like the *Caprichos* and *Disparates,* the "Black Paintings" reveal some of Goya's uncanny observations of human folly in action. But more than that, they expose his intense awareness of the dark forces of panic, terror, fear, hysteria —the all too real ingredients of the human experience.

Against a peaceful, rustic backdrop, two men cudgel each other mercilessly in this painting from the upper room of La Quinta del Sordo. The combatants, one badly bloodied, are knee-deep in a quagmire, unable to escape each other and fated to continue for all eternity their brutal rain of blows. Perhaps their hideous predicament symbolized the fratricidal civil war that Goya had witnessed.

Fight With Clubs, c. 1820-1823

173

NEXT PAGE: Called *Fantastic Vision,* this is one of the most puzzling of the "Black Paintings." Two giant figures hover over a group of horsemen while soldiers with rifles aim in their direction. Goya, who more than once illustrated folk tales in his tapestry cartoons, may have recalled a popular legend of three men who arrived on a cloud over Galicia in northeastern Spain, descended, ate a meal and then flew off.

Una Manola

Leocadia. She was said to be loud and shrill, but perhaps because Goya was deaf he painted her as a tranquil lady leisurely leaning on an iron railing. *Judith (above, right)* is in remarkable contrast. The painting is based on a Biblical

Judith

story; like *Saturn*, it is one of only two "Black Paintings" with a traditional theme. In the tale, the Jewish widow Judith volunteers to save her people by murdering Holofernes, an Assyrian general set on their destruction.

In the painting, Judith, with the help of a servant, is about to dispatch the general, who lies in a drunken stupor at her feet. The determination of Judith's face provides a sharp counterpoint to the demure visage of the *manola*.

Goya was obsessed by the transformation of individuals when they joined together and became a mob. An earlier version of a *Witches' Sabbath (page 84)* is lighthearted, theatrical. According to ancient beliefs, such a sabbath was a meeting of witches presided over by the devil, who frequently appeared in the form of a goat. These sabbaths were pagan orgies of drinking, dancing and singing that convened at sunset and adjourned at dawn. In Goya's first version, the colors were light, the goat's horn bedecked with vine leaves. In the lower room of his country house, however, the elderly Goya painted a scene *(below)* overlaid with gloom, superstition and presentiments of evil; the goat speaks to an assemblage of witches and warlocks, semihumans with hollow eyes and exaggerated faces. Only the young girl in black holding a muff sitting at far

The most powerful—and terrifying—of the "Black Paintings" shows the mythological god Saturn tearing apart one of his young sons. Saturn, the Roman counterpart of the Greek Chronos, was the father of many gods. However, fearing the prophecy that a son would overthrow him, he swallowed them one by one. Only Jupiter, whose mother hid him, survived. Saturn's ferocious cannibalism was the subject of several paintings by old masters, notably one by Rubens, which Goya may have seen in the King's collection. None of the earlier paintings can match Goya's in savagery and passion.

So bizarre and grotesque are *Saturn* and the merrymakers at San Isidro *(left)* that they seem to be the final expression of a mind threatened by madness. But after Goya abandoned his country retreat in 1824 to settle and eventually die in Bordeaux, he continued to work, and in a different mood. There, he made powerful lithographs of bulls *(page 160),* affectionate portraits of friends and a delicate evocation of youth, the *Milkmaid of Bordeaux.* To his dying day, he continued to capture the colors of life as well as the shadows of death.

Saturn Devouring His Son

Artists of Goya's Era

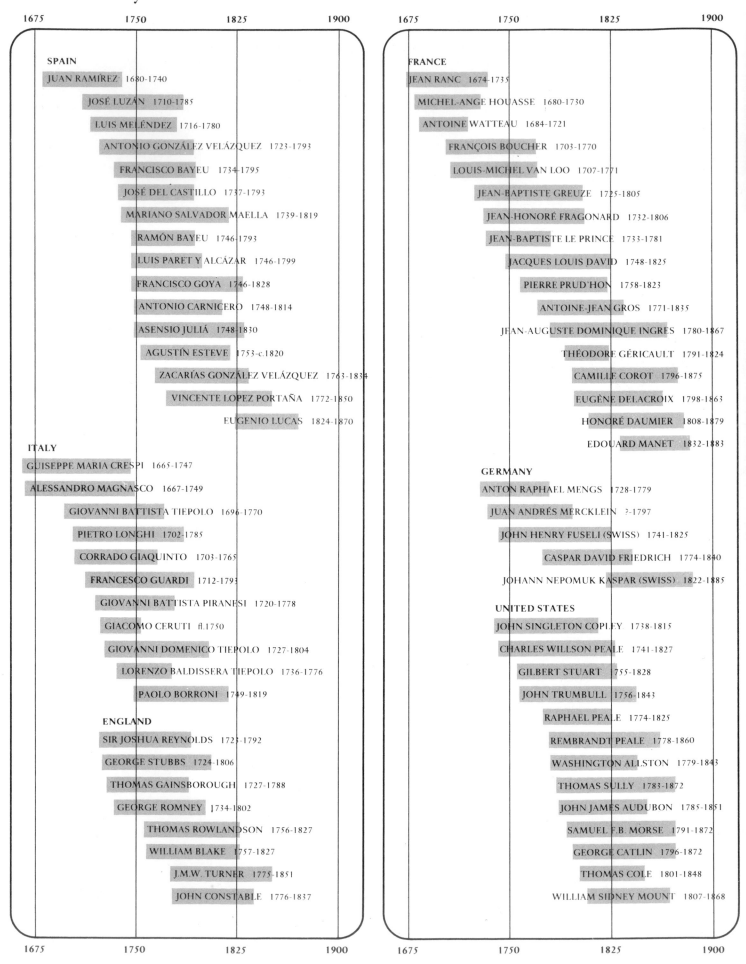

	1675	1750	1825	1900

SPAIN
JUAN RAMÍREZ 1680-1740
JOSÉ LUZÁN 1710-1785
LUIS MELÉNDEZ 1716-1780
ANTONIO GONZÁLEZ VELÁZQUEZ 1723-1793
FRANCISCO BAYEU 1734-1795
JOSÉ DEL CASTILLO 1737-1793
MARIANO SALVADOR MAELLA 1739-1819
RAMÓN BAYEU 1746-1793
LUIS PARET Y ALCÁZAR 1746-1799
FRANCISCO GOYA 1746-1828
ANTONIO CARNICERO 1748-1814
ASENSIO JULIÁ 1748-1830
AGUSTÍN ESTEVE 1753-c.1820
ZACARÍAS GONZÁLEZ VELÁZQUEZ 1763-1834
VINCENTE LOPEZ PORTAÑA 1772-1850
EUGENIO LUCAS 1824-1870

ITALY
GUISEPPE MARIA CRESPI 1665-1747
ALESSANDRO MAGNASCO 1667-1749
GIOVANNI BATTISTA TIEPOLO 1696-1770
PIETRO LONGHI 1702-1785
CORRADO GIAQUINTO 1703-1765
FRANCESCO GUARDI 1712-1793
GIOVANNI BATTISTA PIRANESI 1720-1778
GIACOMO CERUTI fl.1750
GIOVANNI DOMENICO TIEPOLO 1727-1804
LORENZO BALDISSERA TIEPOLO 1736-1776
PAOLO BORRONI 1749-1819

ENGLAND
SIR JOSHUA REYNOLDS 1723-1792
GEORGE STUBBS 1724-1806
THOMAS GAINSBOROUGH 1727-1788
GEORGE ROMNEY 1734-1802
THOMAS ROWLANDSON 1756-1827
WILLIAM BLAKE 1757-1827
J.M.W. TURNER 1775-1851
JOHN CONSTABLE 1776-1837

FRANCE
JEAN RANC 1674-1735
MICHEL-ANGE HOUASSE 1680-1730
ANTOINE WATTEAU 1684-1721
FRANÇOIS BOUCHER 1703-1770
LOUIS-MICHEL VAN LOO 1707-1771
JEAN-BAPTISTE GREUZE 1725-1805
JEAN-HONORÉ FRAGONARD 1732-1806
JEAN-BAPTISTE LE PRINCE 1733-1781
JACQUES LOUIS DAVID 1748-1825
PIERRE PRUD'HON 1758-1823
ANTOINE-JEAN GROS 1771-1835
JEAN-AUGUSTE DOMINIQUE INGRES 1780-1867
THÉODORE GÉRICAULT 1791-1824
CAMILLE COROT 1796-1875
EUGÈNE DELACROIX 1798-1863
HONORÉ DAUMIER 1808-1879
EDOUARD MANET 1832-1883

GERMANY
ANTON RAPHAEL MENGS 1728-1779
JUAN ANDRÉS MERCKLEIN ?-1797
JOHN HENRY FUSELI (SWISS) 1741-1825
CASPAR DAVID FRIEDRICH 1774-1840
JOHANN NEPOMUK KASPAR (SWISS) 1822-1885

UNITED STATES
JOHN SINGLETON COPLEY 1738-1815
CHARLES WILLSON PEALE 1741-1827
GILBERT STUART 1755-1828
JOHN TRUMBULL 1756-1843
RAPHAEL PEALE 1774-1825
REMBRANDT PEALE 1778-1860
WASHINGTON ALLSTON 1779-1843
THOMAS SULLY 1783-1872
JOHN JAMES AUDUBON 1785-1851
SAMUEL F.B. MORSE 1791-1872
GEORGE CATLIN 1796-1872
THOMAS COLE 1801-1848
WILLIAM SIDNEY MOUNT 1807-1868

	1675	1750	1825	1900

Goya's predecessors, contemporaries and successors are grouped chronologically according to country. The bands correspond to the life-spans of the artists.

Bibliography

*Paperback

GOYA—HIS LIFE AND WORK

Beruete y Moret. Aureliano de. *Goya as a Portrait Painter.* Translated from the Spanish by Selwyn Brinton. Houghton Mifflin Co., 1922.

Gassier. Pierre. *Goya: Biographical and Critical Study.* Translated by James Emmons. Editions d'Art Albert Skira. Geneva. 1955.

Gudiol. José. *Goya.* The Library of Great Painters. Harry N. Abrams, Inc., Publishers, 1964.

Harris. Tomás. *Goya: Engravings and Lithographs* (2 vols.). Bruno Cassirer. Oxford, 1964.

Huxley. Aldous. *The Complete Etchings of Goya.* Crown Publishers. 1943.

Klingender. F. D., *Goya in the Democratic Tradition.* Sidgwick and Jackson Ltd., London, 1948.

Lafuente Ferrari. Enrique. *Antecedentes, Coincidencias e Influencias del Arte de Goya* (illustrated catalogue). Talleres de Blass, Madrid. 1947.

Goya: His Complete Etchings, Aquatints, and Lithographs. Harry N. Abrams. Inc., Publishers, 1962.

Goya: The Frescos in San Antonio de la Florida in Madrid. Published under the patronage of the Royal Academy of Fine Arts of San Fernando. Editions d'Art Albert Skira. Geneva. 1955.

López-Rey. José. *A Cycle of Goya's Drawings: The Expression of Truth and Liberty.* The Macmillan Company. 1956.

Francisco de Goya. Masters of Painting. Harper's Art Library. Harper & Row Publishers. 1950.

Goya's Caprichos (2 vols.). Princeton University Press. 1953.

Malraux. André. *Saturn: An Essay on Goya.* Phaidon Publishers Inc., 1957.

Mayer. August L., *Francisco de Goya.* English translation by Robert West. J. M. Dent. London. 1924.

Nordström. Folke. *Goya, Saturn and Melancholy: Studies in the Art of Goya.* Almqvist & Wiksell. Stockholm. 1962.

Sánchez Cantón. Francisco Javier. *Goya.* Reynal & Company. 1964.

The Life and Works of Goya. English translation by Paul Burns. Editorial Peninsular. S.A., Madrid. 1964.

Trapier. Elizabeth du Gué. *Goya and His Sitters: A Study of his Style as a Portraitist.* The Hispanic Society of America. 1964.

Wehle. Harry B., *Fifty Drawings by Francisco Goya.* The Metropolitan Museum of Art. Papers. No. 7. 1938.

ART-HISTORICAL BACKGROUND

Jedlicka. Gotthard. *Spanish Painting.* A Studio Book. The Viking Press. Inc., 1964.

Kimball. Sidney Fiske. *The Creation of the Rococo.* The Philadelphia Museum of Art. 1943.

Kubler. George and Martin S. Soria. *Art and Architecture in Spain and Portugal and Their American Dominions, 1500-1800.* The Pelican History of Art Series. Penguin Books. Inc.. 1959.

Levey. Michael. *Rococo to Revolution: Major Trends in Eighteenth-Century Paintings.** Praeger World of Art Series. Frederick A. Praeger. Publishers. 1966.

López-Rey. José. *Velazquez, A Catalogue Raisonné of his Oeuvre.* Faber & Faber. London. 1963.

Morassi. Antonio. *A Complete Catalogue of the Painting of G. B. Tiepolo* (including pictures by his pupils and followers wrongly attributed to him). Phaidon Publishers Inc., 1962.

G. B. Tiepolo: His Life and Work. Phaidon Publishers Inc., 1955.

Novotny. Fritz. *Painting and Sculpture in Europe, 1780-1880.* The Pelican History of Art Series. Penguin Books. Inc.. 1960.

Trapier. Elizabeth du Gué. *Velasquez.* The Hispanic Society of America. 1948.

Wehle. Harry B., *Great Paintings From the Prado Museum.* With a foreword by F. J. Sánchez Cantón. Harry N. Abrams, Inc., Publishers, 1963.

CULTURAL AND HISTORICAL BACKGROUND

Atkinson. William C., *A History of Spain and Portugal.** Pelican Books Inc., 1965.

Brenan. Gerald. *The Literature of the Spanish People.* Cambridge University Press. Cambridge. 1953 (Also paperback. Meridian Books. 1960).

Carr. Raymond. *Spain 1808-1939.* The Oxford History of Modern Europe. Oxford University Press. London. 1966.

Chapman. Charles E., *A History of Spain.* Founded on the *Historia de España y de la Civilización Española* of Rafael Altamira. The Macmillan Company. 1954.

Coulton. G. G., *Inquisition and Liberty.** Beacon Press. 1959.

Davies. R. Trevor. *The Golden Century of Spain: 1501-1621.* Macmillan & Co., Ltd.. London. 1954.

Diaz-Plaja. Fernando. *The Spaniard and the Seven Deadly Sins.* Charles Scribner's Sons. 1967.

Earl of Ilchester (editor). *The Spanish Journal of Elizabeth Lady Holland.* Longmans. Green. and Co.. London. 1910.

Gay. Peter. *The Enlightenment: An Interpretation.* Alfred A. Knopf. 1966.

Kamen. Henry. *The Spanish Inquisition.* The New American Library. 1966.

Kany. Charles E., *Life and Manners in Madrid: 1750-1800.* University of California Press. 1932.

Livermore. Harold. *A History of Spain.* Farrar. Straus and Cudahy. 1958.

Michener. James A., *Iberia: Spanish Travels and Reflections.* Random House. Inc., 1968.

Morris. James. *The Presence of Spain.* Photographs by Evelyn Hofer. Harcourt. Brace & World. Inc., 1964.

Oliveira. A. Ramos. *Politics, Economics and Men of Modern Spain: 1808-1946.* Translated by Teener Hall. Victor Gollancz Ltd.. London. 1946.

Smith. Bradley. *Spain: A History in Art.* Simon and Schuster. 1966.

Picture Credits

The sources for the illustrations appear below. Credits for pictures from left to right are separated by semicolons, from top to bottom by dashes.

SLIPCASE
Derek Bayes
END PAPERS
Augusto Meneses

CHAPTER 1: 6—Courtesy Museum of Fine Arts, Boston. 10, 11—Ken Kay. 12 —Map by Rafael Palacios. 15—Foto Mas. 17—Lee Boltin; Robert S. Crandall—Lee Boltin; Augusto Meneses; Virginia Meadows Museum—Lee Boltin; The Metropolitan Museum of Art. 18, 19, 20—Lee Boltin. 21— Virginia Meadows Museum. 22, 23—Augusto Meneses. 24—Robert S. Crandall. 25—The Metropolitan Museum of Art. 26, 27—Lee Boltin.

CHAPTER 2: 28—Lee Boltin. 30—Foto Mas. 35—Manso. 41—Augusto Meneses. 42—Manso. 43, 44—Lee Boltin. 45—Giraudon. 46—Courtesy Museum of Fine Arts, Boston. 47—Manso.

CHAPTER 3: 48—Manso. 51—Augusto Meneses. 52, 53—Foto Mas. 56— Augusto Meneses. 61—Augusto Meneses. 62, 63—Scala. 64—Lee Boltin. 65—National Gallery of Art, Washington, D.C. 66—Frank Lerner. 67—The Hispanic Society of America. 68, 69—Lee Boltin. 70, 71 —Collection of Mrs. Mellon Bruce—Augusto Meneses; Lee Boltin. 72-75 —Augusto Meneses.

CHAPTER 4: 76—Lee Boltin. 79—Photographie Bulloz. 81—Foto Mas. 84 —Augusto Meneses. 86—Foto Mas. 89—Augusto Meneses. 91-95—

Augusto Meneses.

CHAPTER 5: 96—Augusto Meneses. 102, 103—Foto Mas. 107—Photographie Bulloz. 109—Courtesy Museum of Fine Arts, Boston. 110—Lee Boltin except bottom right courtesy Museum of Fine Arts, Boston. 111— Left courtesy Museum of Fine Arts, Boston (2); right Lee Boltin (2). 112— Lee Boltin except bottom right courtesy Museum of Fine Arts, Boston. 113 —Lee Boltin. 114—Courtesy Museum of Fine Arts, Boston (2)—Lee Boltin (2). 115-119—Lee Boltin.

CHAPTER 6: 120—The Metropolitan Museum of Art. 122—New York Public Library. 123—Foto Mas. 126, 127—Courtesy of the Art Institute of Chicago. 129, 130, 131—Lee Boltin. 132-135—Augusto Meneses. 136 —Larry Burrows. 137—Augusto Meneses. 138, 139—Courtesy Museum of Fine Arts, Boston. 140—Augusto Meneses—Courtesy Museum of Fine Arts, Boston. 141—Courtesy Museum of Fine Arts, Boston—Augusto Meneses. 142, 143—Courtesy Museum of Fine Arts, Boston.

CHAPTER 7: 144—The Hispanic Society of America. 146—Foto Mas. 148— Foto Mas. 149—Lee Boltin. 150—Museu de Arte de São Paulo. 153— Foto Mas. 157—Lee Boltin. 158—Courtesy Museum of Fine Arts, Boston. 159—Lee Boltin. 160—Courtesy Museum of Fine Arts, Boston. 161—Lee Boltin. 162, 163—The National Gallery of Art, Washington, D.C.

CHAPTER 8: 164—Lee Boltin. 166—Foto Mas. 167—The Minneapolis Institute of Arts. 168—Foto Mas. 171—Lee Boltin. 173-185—Lee Boltin.

Acknowledgments

José Camon Aznar, Director, Museo Lázaro Galiano, Madrid; Claude Brenot, C.N.R.S., Cabinet des Médailles, Paris; Cathedral Chapter, Cathedral of Toledo; Cathedral Chapter, Cathedral of Valencia; Cathedral Chapter, Cathedral of Zaragoza; Guillermo Guastavino Gallen, Director, Biblioteca Nacional, Madrid; Colta Ives, The Metropolitan Museum of Art; Stephanie Loeb, Boston Museum of Fine Arts; Yves Metman, Conservateur aux Archives Nationales, Paris; Carlos Ruspoli y Caro, Duque de Sueca y Marquese de Boadilla, Florence and Madrid; Xavier de Salas, Assistant Director, Museo Nacional del Prado, Madrid; Francisco Javier Sánchez Cantón, Director, Museo Nacional del Prado, Madrid; Maria del Rosario Cayetana Fitz James Stuart y Silva, Duchess of Alba de Tormes, Palace of Liria, Madrid; Luisa Isabel Alvarez de Toledo y Maura, Duchess of Medina Sidonia, Palace of Medina Sidonia, Sanlúcar de Barrameda.

Index

Numerals in italics indicate a picture of the subject mentioned. Unless otherwise identified, all listed art works are by Goya. Dimensions are given in inches; height precedes width.